CU00692565

(RASPBERRY PI 3 and VISUAL BASIC)
Programming Windows 10 IoT Core

Version 1 Revision 2

ISBN-13: 978-0692071885
ISBN-10: 0692071881

Published by A1 Entities, Inc. (a1entities.com)

Printed by Amazon

Editor: Joey Johnson

Associate Editor: Casey Kimberley

Technical Editor: Gary Wensink

Dedication

I want to remember my Grandmother who always encouraged us all to "never stop learning, no matter your age."

A special thanks to my family, especially Carole and Zach for encouraging me to write and finish this book, and then having the patience to allow me the time required.

Foreword by the Author

I had not worked with the Raspberry Pi computer very long when I realized how much fun it could be. Like most, I started with Python, used Scratch, and some of the music software on Raspbian (default operating system for the Raspberry Pi).

After a few successful projects, I grew tired of Python and the limitations of the GUI in Tkinter. I do not mean knock Python at all. I want to do more in the future with Python. It was just too long of a learning curve for the GUI language part. I felt Visual Basic (VB) might prove to be more efficient and faster for my projects.

Being an old Visual Basic guy, and having interest in the electronics and other aspects of the Pi, I wanted quicker results. I started out trying to learn C Sharp better, and I probably will spend more time there in the future, but again it was taking too long to learn. I wanted to utilize some of the existing knowledge I had in Visual Basic, if possible.

I found some information was on the internet, but it is all over the place for the Pi and Windows 10 IoT (Internet of Things). After doing a few weeks of research, I decided to use Visual Basic in Visual Studio Community 2017. I wanted to see how feasible Visual Basic or VB still is for the Raspberry Pi and Windows 10 IoT.

I picked a project to develop in Visual Basic and utilized the Pi Foundations 7" Raspberry touchscreen. This screen allowed me to keep my PC screens for work.

After more research and coding, I found out my project was viable and perfect for Visual Basic. I created a speech timer application for my local

Toastmasters club and presented it at one of the meetings. It worked well.

After finishing this initial test project, I was inspired to write about everything I had learned and wanted to explore this further. I started that process, and after gathering more information, I decided to present it in a book for others. The fantastic little Raspberry Pi computer and Windows 10 IoT are an incredible combination for your projects.

I wanted to provide information to interest a novice to learn more, and possibly provide something a veteran could use to get past any hurdles they might have with the Raspberry Pi and Visual Basic. This book is meant to help both.

I carefully chose the projects that are presented in the book. There are fundamental examples of Visual Basic's buttons, textboxes, progress bars, textblocks, file access, and even some SQL Server examples.

I could have gone a lot deeper in electronics, but did not. The Raspberry Pi computer has a GPIO-General Purpose Input Output or electronics capability. Instead, I choose to just scratch the surface in electronics and cover what might make people interested in the Raspberry Pi.

A genuine electronic enthusiast will know how to wire or configure a 555 timer, sensors, or a circuit. I do feel there is a lot of confusion as to how the Raspberry Pi's GPIO is setup and how to use it. I chose to try to clarify this GPIO setup, and provide simple examples of input and output electronics pins.

I think it is unfortunate that Microsoft has chosen to go to C# or C Sharp so exclusively. I have not seen much that Visual Studio using a CLR-Common Language Runtime cannot do using Visual Basic. Examples are becoming rarer and rarer though for Visual Basic, and this is especially true in the Universal or UWP-Universal Windows Programming arena.

Microsoft has a language with Visual Basic that most programmers for the last 20 years can use and understand. The user base is enormous, and Microsoft has chosen to go in another direction. Oh well!

Visual Basic does work with the Raspberry Pi, and it works well for Windows 10 IoT programming. It is too bad Xamarin and Visual Studio Community did not provide the ability to use Visual Basic for Android and IOS instead of C#. I programmed Android with Android Studio instead of Visual Studio since it only works in C sharp using Xamarin. You must learn Java anyway, and that was the bulk of the code required.

I hope you enjoy using this book and the samples in Visual Basic and the Raspberry Pi computer. It is a neat device and has many capabilities.

Author's Background

Carl Shackelford currently lives in Pensacola, Florida on Perdido Key with his wife Carole and their dog Todd. He has been involved in technology most of his career.

He started his career learning electronics and computers at Dyersburg State Community College where he had a dual major with an Associate of Science in Industrial Electronics and an Associate of Science in Computer Technology.

Carl worked as an Electronics and Computer Technician for several years early in his career. He continued his education and earned a BS/MS from Middle Tennessee State University in Industrial Studies (EE Tech now) Minoring in Computer Science. Some of his graduate courses were in Technical education, robotics, data structures, and circuit design.

Carl has worked in programming and engineering with well-known companies like Nissan, Cummins, TRW, NFIB, Deloitte & Touché, Rehau, and Alto. During this time, he completed Microsoft's MCP, MCSD, MCSP, and MCT-Microsoft Certified Trainer certifications, and was certified in the Microsoft Train the Trainer program.

The last few years he has been working as the Founder/CEO of two companies: PSI/A1 Barcode Systems and A1 Entities, Inc. He is currently working for Bar Code Integrators, Inc. in several roles.

For fun, he loves to fish and golf. At the time of this writing, he is serving as the Area 55 Director of Toastmasters in Florida.

Carl has always had a love for technology and has always been interested in teaching and sharing it with others.

Table of Contents

Disclaimer

Visual Studio and Visual Studio Community are owned by Microsoft.

The Raspberry Pi and associated products are owned by the Raspberry Pi Foundation. The Pi Academy and JAM outings are organizations and outings setup by the Raspberry Pi Foundation.

Fritzing is a great foundation that provides breadboard and schematic software. All drawings for breadboard and schematics were made available due to the Fritzing product. Join the Fritzing Foundation and contribute a small donation.

This book is in no way endorsed or approved by Microsoft, Raspberry Pi Foundation, CanaKit, Sunfounder, or Fritzing. I just used these technologies to provide the solutions for the book.

CanaKit donated units for me to test, and were very helpful with anything I needed. Many thanks to them.

Cana Kit Always, start with a CanaKit.

Purpose of this Book

This book was written to consolidate information regarding the Raspberry Pi using Windows 10 IoT and Visual Basic in one place. Whether a self-study guide or a classroom teaching resource, this book will make a particularly useful resource for young computer enthusiast and experienced programmers getting started in Pi Development.

More people seem to be able to understand and complete code projects quicker with Visual Basic. I think it will be a welcome book in the absence of Visual Basic examples or instruction on the web.

This book starts someone from ground zero, and without going into all the twist and turns of development, gently takes you into Visual Basic and the tools you need for development. The book progresses from this beginning to simple projects. The projects are deliberately simple, and all code is provided in the book in gray blocks.

The first project shows merely a Hello, Pi on the screen. The second project expands on the first project adding a button input on the screen.

The Dispatch Timer was introduced to show someone how to use delays and counters and timers with your projects. The timer object will be used on several projects.

We then progress into electronics and using simple input and outputs. Previous electronic experience is not required. This part covers electronic inputs and outputs, so it is the basics of all future electronics projects. The next project expands by adding an electronic pushbutton with the previous project.

We then progress into file access and writing and reading, which is a skill any programmer needs to know.

The last project shows how to connect to and send SQL Statements to a Microsoft SQL Server database, and how to handle the return information.

Each project is likely the foundation for a future project. The projects are designed to teach you what you need to know to invent something and give you the confidence to learn more on your own.

This is a book of smaller projects that can be combined to create your project.

Stock Raspberry Pi 3 B Board as printed on the board above.

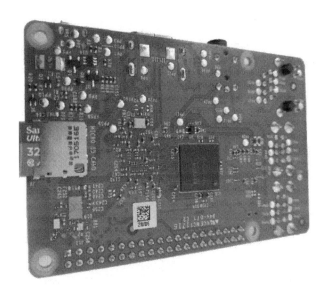

The back side of the Pi 3 B Board

Pi Zero Board W front with US Coins for perspective.

Pi Zero W Back with Keyboard Perspective.

Raspberry Pi Boards

Note: The microSD chip does not come with the board nor do the heat sinks. I suggest you order those in a kit if all the parts needed are not something you have available. The CanaKit is a great kit to package the Raspberry Pi and provide those components.

The **Pi** as I will call it through the book is the Raspberry Pi board or computer created by the Raspberry Pi Foundation.

For these this book, I suggest using the Raspberry Pi 3 B board. I am not suggesting the other boards the Pi Foundation has are not capable. The Raspberry Pi 3 B just has the most ports and power available for projects and testing.

The Pi Zero board is fantastic when a smaller computer is required. You can do all development on your Raspberry Pi 3 B board, and use the Pi Zero board when you deploy your project. If it is an electronic project, the PI Zero will require soldering.

Read the specifications of all the boards before deciding on the final board to use for your project. Less power consumption, size, and need for wireless may all be factors. There is a Zero board with Wi-Fi and without. Be sure you need Wi-Fi and if not go with the non-W series of Pi Zero board. New versions are coming out all the time, so review the Raspberry Pi Foundation site.

Do remember, different cases and parts might are needed for each board version. It is much safer to have a case or kit to protect your Pi computer. CanaKit does a great job of providing kits for most versions or Raspberry Pi.

The History of the Raspberry Pi

The Raspberry Pi was created by the Raspberry Pi Foundation to promote the teaching of robotics and basic computer science in schools and for developing countries in 2012. The Raspberry Pi is a single board computer created in the United Kingdom. The boards are manufactured in a Sony Factory in Pencoed, Wales.

As of this writing, over 17 million Pi Computers have sold. The first release was a Raspberry PI 1 Model, and the Model A. A cheaper version came out later.

As of this writing, the pricing is currently $5-$35 depending on the Raspberry Pi model, for the board only. The Foundation has released many versions, since the initial Pi board release. The latest major Raspberry Pi computers released are the Pi 3 Model B+, Pi 3 Model B, Pi Zero, and the Pi Zero W.

Today you might find a Raspberry Pi anywhere. The Pi computers are used in manufacturing, digital signage, retro games, weather stations, security systems, and kiosk to name a few.

There are hundreds of Raspberry Pi Academy certified educators. The UK still has the bulk of the education classes on the Raspberry Pi. There are user's groups (Jams), college courses, courses (Pi Academy), and more for the Pi community. Most of this information is provided at www.raspberrypi.org.

Raspberry Pi Board Models
https://www.raspberrypi.org/products/

What Makes Up A PI?

The Raspberry Pi 3 B+ is the latest Raspberry Pi with the most features. It has a 1.4 GHz 64 bit quad-core Arm processor, 1 GIG of RAM, 4 USB 2.0 ports, microSD slot, GPIO, Ethernet-RJ45, DSI Port, Bluetooth 4.1, Wi-Fi 802.11n, HDMI, 15-pin MIPI Camera connector, Stereo out, and USB boot capabilities.   Raspberry Pi 3 B+ is most full-featured Pi you can buy, as of this writing.

The Raspberry Pi 3 B+ is the newest computer and the one I suggest you start with, even if you migrate to the cheaper PI Zero or PI Zero W later. I suggest you have one of these to do testing. This PI 3 B+ unit has the most features and speed available in a PI, as of this writing.

The Raspberry PI Zero comes in two primary configurations. They cost $5 and $10 currently. The main difference is the W unit has Wi-Fi. Both can support HDMI out, but require an adapter since only a MINI HDMI is provided. It also has a Micro USB port and not a full USB port. The Raspberry Pi Zero may be perfectly suitable and even preferable for your final project due to its lower power requirements and smaller footprint. I highly suggest starting with the Pi 3 B+ though, since it has an RJ45 Ethernet jack and all the ports that make testing and data transfers faster and easier.

None of the Raspberry Pi Models have a built-in Real-Time Clock, but there are components you can add a battery backup that can accomplish this. They can and frequently do connect to a network time server for time accuracy, if available. Time is not saved on the standard unit and time resets at boot.

There are many cases and kits from CanaKit and others that are on the market that can be used with your Raspberry Pi if your project requires them.

(From Wikipedia)
https://en.wikipedia.org/wiki/Raspberry_Pi

GPIO

GPIO General Purpose Input & Output (Electronics)

Electronic signals and their input/output on the Raspberry Pi, seem to be what most people have interest in. The Raspberry Pi is used to light up LEDs, turn on motors, and even interface with robotics. The Raspberry Pi is a place where you can also do all the cool robotics things that require electronics input and output and a computer.

I will give you the libraries, a few samples, and explain GPIO so you can start your journey. You can take your experimentation where you want. The Raspberry Pi has even been in space, so where you go is endless.

Be careful; any project working with the GPIO does have the possibility of frying your Raspberry Pi. Always, **always**, turn off power before doing anything. If you smell burning and it smells like silicone or electronics assume it is burning and **POWER IT OFF IMMEDIATELY**.

On the following page is a diagram of the Raspberry Pi 3 B that will help guide us through the setups.

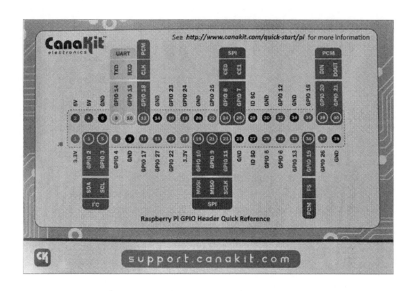

The CanaKit Raspberry Pi GPIO Connector Pinout.

The Raspberry Pi 3 B and PI Zero have a 40-pin pinout. Some of the older Raspberry Pi's do too, but we will only show examples of the Raspberry Pi 3 B and B+.

Above is the GPIO representation of the Raspberry Pi. CanaKit does a great job of kitting components with the Pi, and make it much easier to get started. This pinout card typically comes with their kits.

Note: Raspberry Pi 1 Models A and B have only a 26 pin GPIO. We are not going to discuss these older boards, and our Pi 3 B will have 40 pins as pictured.

GPIO#	2nd func.	Pin#	Pin#	2nd fun.	GPIO#
	+3.3 V	1	2	+5 V	
2	SDA1 (I²C)	3	4	+5 V	
3	SCL1 (I²C)	5	6	GND	
4	GCLK	7	8	TXD0 (UART)	14
	GND	9	10	RXD0 (UART)	15
17	GEN0	11	12	GEN1	18
27	GEN2	13	14	GND	
22	GEN3	15	16	GEN4	23
	+3.3 V	17	18	GEN5	24
10	MOSI (SPI)	19	20	GND	
9	MISO (SPI)	21	22	GEN6	25
11	SCLK (SPI)	23	24	CE0_N (SPI)	8
	GND	25	26	CE1_N (SPI)	7
	(Pi 1 Models A and B stop here)				
EEPROM	ID_SD	27	28	ID_SC	EEPROM
5	N/A	29	30	GND	
6	N/A	31	32		12
13	N/A	33	34	GND	
19	N/A	35	36	N/A	16
26	N/A	37	38	Digital IN	20
	GND	39	40	Digital OUT	21

Note: GPIO numbers are not the same as the pins dictated on the Pin Numbers. Be sure to use the GPIO#'s when doing any wiring. These are the basics of the Raspberry Pi Architecture and the features that are available. This is available in much more detail on the internet and at raspberrypi.org.

I do not want to include information that is readily available online if it is not directly related to our programming needs in the book.

Operating Systems

The Raspberry Pi Foundation has a version of Linux called Raspbian that runs very well. I started with this, and have one Raspberry Pi setup with this OS-Operating System. It has excellent tools for those who want to use Python, Scratch, and the other standard programming tools. I have heard there is a software tool for Visual Basic that will allow it to run on Raspbian, but that is another book.

Raspbian is exceptionally efficient and has all the Office type tools that could make it practical to utilize as your only computer. I usually use Python and Tkinter, if I use Raspbian. The GUI-Graphic User Interface part is a bit cumbersome, but the language is relatively straightforward. The Python programming language even works on the Microsoft Visual Studio IDE, but Python 2.6 itself does not provide many tools to assist you in GUI development. I have heard there are some GUI tools you can use outside of Microsoft Visual Studio that can be helpful.

Here are a few of the Operating Systems used on the Raspberry Pi as follows: Raspbian, 9front, Android Things, Arch Linux ARM, CentOS, Debian, FreeBSD, Gentoo Linux, Ubuntu Core, and Slackware. The OS or Operating System we will use in this book will be Microsoft Windows 10 Iot Core. Core means all the features of Windows 10 IoT are not available.

Disclaimer and Precautions

Although everything in this book has been validated and checked on numerous Raspberry Pi 3 B units, there is still a chance that you could have issues. Static electricity, bad circuits and components, and wiring the wrong pins or the like could cause your board to fry and likewise can cause you harm.

Some advanced projects require an engineer or electrician to understand the dangers and precautions that should be taken. I left this kind of projects out of the book. You should not attempt anything beyond the electronic examples this book, without an electrician or someone experienced in electrical circuits or electronics.

We assume no liability for the wiring or application of our samples. We will not replace boards, components, or accept responsibility for damages that might occur when you are trying our sample applications. Anyone in electronics realizes the threat of static and lack of proper electronic gear (like ground straps), and how easy it is to end up with a failed board or component.

This book is meant to be a primer to help get you started in Visual Basic with Visual Studio Community and Windows 10 IoT and the Pi.

Components for the Pi

Many components are available for the Raspberry Pi at a reasonable price. The Raspberry Pi can be utilized by itself to do most of these projects. The Pi by itself is just a computer board. I have the required components listed below that will protect your Pi, and make it easier and more fun to use.

I also included the recommended components that are nice to have. Your direction and projects will dictate what you need. There are not a lot of components required for this book. I suggest you buy parts as you need them for your projects.

Naturally, you can create switches (jumper wires), and a volt-ohm meter can be used to test the electrical components for the results instead of some of the components.

Required Components

The required products for this book are the Raspberry Pi 3 B Board, USB Keyboard & Mouse, WI-FI/Ethernet, 2 Heat Sinks, Recommended Power Supply (usually a 2-amp 5-volt minimum USB Micro supply), HDMI Cable, NOOBs OS, Windows 10 Computer, and a copy of Visual Studio 2017 Community or newer.

A 220-ohm resistor, LED that is rated for a 220 ohms resistor, breadboard, push-button switch, and jumper wires are the only additional items that are required. CanaKit has a nice kit with all of these.

You will need some type of monitor on your Raspberry Pi if you do not purchase the 7" touchscreen. Most monitors with HDMI connection will work fine.

Recommended Components

The products mentioned here are recommended to do the projects. I also suggest the 7" screen and case that the Raspberry PI Foundation recommends. If you do not want to go this way I would suggest at minimum buy the case kit built for the Pi. A case for the Pi will nicely expose the ports and GPIO you need.

A switchable power supply is an excellent idea, too. Unplugging and plugging the cable from the Pi creates an excellent chance for static and arching of the power cord, which is never good.

Get a nice kit as mentioned above with at the least a breadboard, ribbon cable, and connectors to hook the GPIO of the PI to the breadboard slots. Some kits have cameras, robotic motors, and a lot more.

The touchscreen kit I have puts the Raspberry Pi board inside a case exposing the GPIO, and dual power, and ribbon cable to connect it. The touchscreen is around $75, and the other kit is $50 or so with electronics components. It makes everything much more accessible.

I like the 7-inch touch screen recommended by the Pi Foundation and the way it houses the Pi board. This one works well. A lot of the HATs with touchscreens will not work with Windows IoT. The touch part does not work for most.

I keep a wireless keyboard/mouse plugged into mine. I use the Logitech K400 Plus, but others I have used work well too. Most touchscreens can be setup to open a keyboard on the screen if your project requires it.

I like the CanaKit case for protecting the Pi computer. This case and components that are around $65 for the Pi 3 B. The Zero boards are cheaper. The CanaKit GPIO extender provides both positive and negative voltage down the side of the board and all the necessary jumper wires and accessories as does SunFounder. Whatever you decide, they are all are on Amazon.

Installing Windows 10 IoT Core

The hard disk default or boot disk is the microSD, usually. The microSD will be the memory and startup disk with the Operating System (OS). The faster the MicroSD, the better. The Foundation had the foresight or maybe experience, to provide a way to start up most of the Operating Systems from one 16 Gig microSD Chip.
https://www.raspberrypi.org/?s=noobs

Most of us should start as newbies and utilize the NOOBS startup disk. It is available on raspberrypi.org in two flavors a full version and a lite version. It also comes loaded on a microSD with a CanaKit order. The NOOBS disk allows you to boot from a few of the primary OS offerings provided and the operating system is then it will be downloaded from the internet. The offering from Pi changes routinely to add more Operating Systems. NOOBs Lite usually is all you need.

When the NOOBs microSD is put in, and an Operating System is selected, it will overwrite the disk with that Operating System. I highly suggest purchasing multiple microSD's and that you keep at least one extra NOOBS microSD just in case. Reinstalling is painless on the Pi if it is required.

Additionally, you will need to have FAT32 formatting on your MicroSD. Sometimes they are formatted that way and sometimes not. Several free tools are out there for Windows 10. Be VERY careful not to overwrite your Micro SD disk unintentionally or your Windows 10 hard drive.

You can also download and set the microSD card up with the latest software for the Windows 10 IoT on Microsoft's site. Here is a link to a video which shows how to start using the Pi Windows 10 IoT version, where they did a pretty good job.

https://www.youtube.com/watch?v=JPRUbGIyODY

It can take several minutes to download. It can also take 2-3 minutes to boot for the first time once inserted into the Pi, so be patient. If this is not enough Microsoft has a site dedicated to Windows IoT Core installations on the Raspberry Pi. You will need to download and copy the files to your microSD after it is formatted.

Again, NOOBS lite usually is all you need from the Raspberry Pi Foundation. Here is a video if all else false
https://www.raspberrypi.org/help/noobs-setup/2/

Here is the Microsoft Download and information site.
https://docs.microsoft.com/en-us/windows/iot-core/getstarted
Download Site
https://developer.microsoft.com/en-us/windows/iot/downloads

Setting Up Your Raspberry Pi

To program your Raspberry PI, you must prepare a microSD. The easiest and recommended way is to utilize your NOOBS microSD chip. Power down your Pi. Put your NOOBS microSD chip into your Raspberry Pi. Then hook up your monitor, mouse, PS, and keyboard.

NOTE: Never pull your microSD chip out without powering down first.

Power on you your Raspberry PI unit by plugging in your power cord(switching power dongles are available on Amazon). A menu will appear in a few minutes that says Windows 10 IoT. If you do not have a backup of your NOOBS SD, you should do so before installing Windows 10 IoT. Note that once Windows 10 IoT is installed, you will have written over NOOBS on this chip. The NOOBS software is on the Raspberry Pi site and can be downloaded to your PC if you need it. This will be nice if you need to setup another microSD chip.

Once you install Windows 10 IoT, you will already have your WI-FI or Ethernet set up. Your IP Address will be on the Raspberry Pi screen after bootup. This IP Address can change. I highly suggest you use wired Ethernet in your setup. Wi-Fi has a few bugs that are a pain for development. I also recommend turning Bluetooth off. Sometimes the password entry into Wi-Fi and other places is affected by Bluetooth being on in setup.

Now you will be ready to continue with the rest of the setup. There are several tools and settings that can be helpful when you start programming.

The Windows 10 IoT Core Dashboard on your Windows 10 machine will be your best tool for setting up your Raspberry Pi from an administrator screen. The Tools chapter that follows will go over this.

Tools for Windows 10 IoT Development

You should go to the Windows site and download Windows IoT Core Dashboard for your Windows 10 development machine. To program your Pi, you will need a Windows 10 or newer machine.

Below is a place you can download it.
https://developer.microsoft.com/en-us/windows/iot/downloads

Install Windows 10 IoT Core Dashboard for your Windows 10 development machine. Windows 10 IoT Core is the only Tool I use to control my Pi remotely for administration.

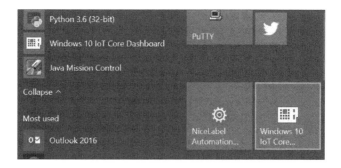

Windows 10 IoT Core Icon for Managing your Pi remotely.

Microsoft Documentation
https://docs.microsoft.com/en-us/windows/iot-core/manage-your-device/deviceportal

The first time the tool is started, it will possibly require these login items. Your Raspberry Pi must be running and on the network.
Administrator: miniwinpc\administrator and Password: p@ssw0rd
If this does not work just use administrator and omit "miniwinpc\".

Usually, the startup machine name will be **miniwinpc**. This is the default.
It can be changed.

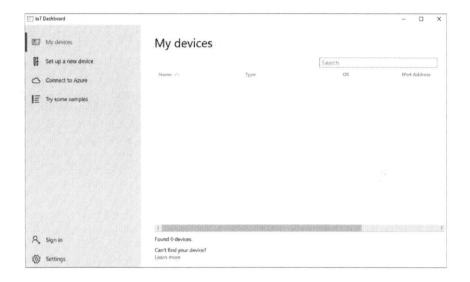

Windows 10 IoT Core Dashboard with no Pi computer found.

Windows 10 IoT Core Dashboard after Device Found at 10.10.2.31

Right-clicking on the **miniwinpc** will bring down a menu as shown in the next image. You may have renamed your computer to something else.

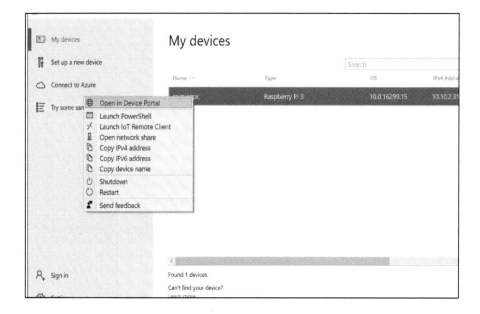

Windows 10 IoT Core – Selection of Open a Device Portal

Once selected you will get a browser screen to the Raspberry Pi's Admin area's web portal. If you need to login you can on the first occurrence, use the default administrator and password.

Administrator: administrator and Password: p@ssw0rd

The actual screen is on the next page is from **Open in Device Portal** after the login has completed.

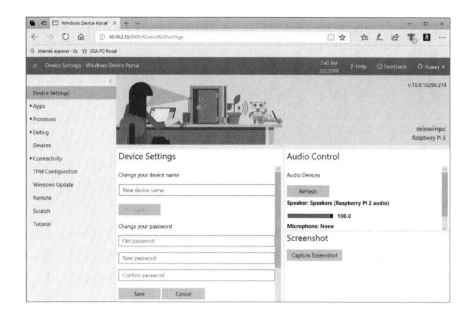

Windows Device Portal: Device Portal for your Pi and Windows 10 IoT OS.

You can change most device settings in the screen above.

You will be able to access the admin screens on your Windows 10 IoT OS. Depending on your settings and login level, they are available from the Pi browser (I never do it this way). This screen will allow setup of Applications and numerous other configurations and things that you will find useful. Managing it all from Windows 10 was much easier.

The managing applications area is likely what you will use the most.

Apps | Apps manager
It will allow you to start and fire up different Foreground and Background applications.

For the Pi, only one GUI Foreground application is available to run at a time, and it has a check beside it if it is running.

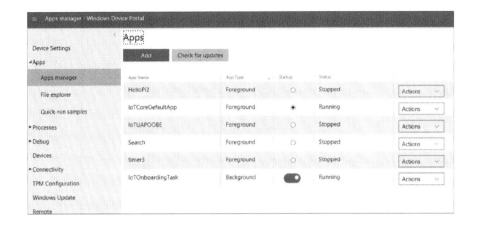

Raspberry Pi Screen that controls apps parameters.

I think the rest is self-explanatory. You can even Quick-Run samples under >**Apps**, and you can look at the Processes and connectivity.

Get the IP Address of your Raspberry Pi; mine is 10.10.2.31.

You can right-click and chose PowerShell too.

Screen after a Right click and choosing Launch PowerShell

Add your password. The default again is p@ssw0rd

PowerShell is probably handy, but you will need a reference to all the commands for PowerShell or a better understanding than I have, to use it. PowerShell is a line command program that many systems administrators use to control remote machines.

Dashboard Control
https://docs.microsoft.com/en-us/windows/iot-core/manage-your-device/remotedisplay

Command Line Utilities
https://docs.microsoft.com/en-us/windows/iot-core/manage-your-device/commandlineutils

Admin Screen Functionality

The admin screen or Windows Device Portal on Windows 10 IoT Core Dashboard was utilized for most of my development. Valuable information about your Pi can only be found and adjusted here. There is a good user interface here. Additionally, if you know all the line commands for PowerShell, you and can use it.

Apps Functionality

Apps functionality can be setup in the Windows Device Portal on Windows 10 IoT Dashboard. Go to **Apps | Apps Manager**. Applications can be setup, restarted, and deleted here. Only one Foreground GUI application can be active at a time, unlike typical windows.

Any application can be set to run upon boot up from this screen. Background applications have no GUI or windows visibility, and you can have more than one running simultaneously. These types of applications are both managed from the Applications area.

All applications that have been tested and debugged from Visual Studio are visible and available on the **Apps** Screen.

This Windows 10 IoT Dashboard is a must. The dashboard allows you to use the Administrator Web Portal or the PowerShell to manage the Raspberry Pi running Windows 10 IoT OS.

Other Information

Many other things are done using the web portal. Processes and many other items can be turned on or off for one. You can also restart your Raspberry Pi from your Windows 10 development computer using the web portal.

Programming and Visual Basic

The examples in this book use the Windows 10 IoT (Internet of Things) Core operating system from Microsoft. It makes sense to use the Microsoft programming tools with a Microsoft environment. The Microsoft compiler takes all languages to a CLR or Common Language Runtime before compiling anyway.

Since all the compiled code from Visual Studio Community 2017 is the same at runtime, why not use the more straightforward language to program. The only reason I see for changing to C Sharp is that more examples are being done it (C#).

The programming environment we are using in this book is Visual Basic. C# or C Sharp knowledge is valuable to know, I agree. You can utilize Visual Basic more effectively with objects and classes if you are familiar with the C# terminology. If you already have C# programming experience, then I highly suggest you continue down that path. This book is a guide for the rest of us. You get both languages (C# and Visual Basic) with the Visual Studio 2017 Community suite of products anyway.

There are a few concepts we will review in the book, to try and help those with absolutely no knowledge of Visual Basic. There are tons of examples out there, and the typical Visual Basic examples will likely run if they contain the same libraries and references. The provided References under references in Visual Studio are Universal and Microsoft.NETCore.UniversalWindowsPlatform (UWP comes from Universal Windows Platform).

These references are found in the **References** section in Visual Studio and Solution Explorer, which we will get to later. There are some limitations and exceptions to Universal. It is not a full set of Windows references and libraries. A few things are missing in the Universal library you might need. This is not unusual since the goal is to keep the binaries small and eliminate compiling anything not customarily used.

This is not meant to be a book to teach you Visual Basic, just a guide to help you get on track with Visual Basic and Visual Studio Community using the Raspberry Pi with Windows 10 IoT Core.

These Visual Basic examples use Visual Studio Community 2017 and update revision (15.15.7), available February 25, 2018. Older versions may require an update to run some of the samples here.

Variables

Variables are all objects with properties and methods. They are mainly used for assigning and holding values.

We will mainly use the variables types below. Again, this is only a brief description of the necessary variables in most of these projects.

These variables are declared as follows:

String
Dim a as string="abcde"

Integer
Dim I as integer=0

Boolean
Dim LightOn as Boolean=true

You can use variables in many ways depending on where they are declared. Variables are locally in a routine if declared there. If they are declared at the top of a class, they are global across the whole class they might be local only to a subroutine or function if re-declared in the subroutine.

Subroutines and Functions

Subroutines and functions allow us to divert our code path when needed. These routines called subroutines and functions must be inside the class we are working with or inside another class included or inherited. This will be simpler than it sounds.

Subs

Private Sub MySub() is all that is required with an End Sub tag.

The code call MySub() is all that is required to redirect code to run this subroutine.

It is created like below.

```
Private Sub MySub (LiteOn as boolean)
End Sub
```

This allows you to pass one or more variables with the routine when it is called. The variable inside the subroutine will be required if the keyword optional is not used.

MySub(true) would be how this would be called. The value of the variable LiteON would only change in the subroutine.

Functions

```
Private Function MyFunctionIs (lite as Boolean, name as string, I as integer) as String
```

Note: A function is like a subroutine but also includes the ability to pass a variable from a function name using a return.

```
Private Function MyFunctionIs(lite as Boolean, name as string, I as integer) as String
```

43

```
        Return "MY STRING IS HERE"

End Function
```

This might be called in the code.

```
Dim s as string=""
s= MyFunctionIs(true,"Joe",22)
```

s would equal "MY STRING IS HERE"

It could also be as follows:

```
Dim s as string=MyFunctionIs(true, "Joe", 22)
```

You will see this in code and sometimes it is calling a library with objects you might not understand. You can explore these objects if you want. It is not required that you to understand more than is necessary to accomplish your task in this book. This is the beauty of Visual Basic and C Sharp(C#).

A typical use of variables in local use.

```
Private sub LiteItUp (mystring as string)
  Mystring="abcd"
End Sub
```

It is a subroutine where a value can be passed when it is called, and it can be changed in the subroutine. The variable's value is only true when it is in the subroutine.

LiteitUp("Pretty Light") is the way a value could be passed and could be called.

```
Private Function LiteItUp (mystring as string) as string
  ABC="abcd"

  If mystring="Pretty Light" then
        Return "It was a Red Light"
  Else
          Return "It was Dark"
  End if

End Function
```

Note: the function can pass back a string with a simple
Return "It was Dark"

This overview is not meant to explain everything you need to know about programming. It is just to get you started. I have more explanations throughout the examples that will probably help you understand these basic concepts even better.

There are many tutorials on the internet about functions, subroutines, objects, variables and Visual Basic. It is mostly the same with Universal Visual Basic, as it is Visual Basic for Windows. Most of those examples will be valid to review for help.

Toolbox Controls

Buttons and Textboxes are our main GUI objects/controls we will use here. These are graphic or GUI-Graphical User Interface objects that have properties and methods and events attached to them. There are properties windows available to set them up in design mode to specific values, but they can have properties that can be changed at runtime, too.

An example is a textbox and its text property.

Textbox1.text="ABCD"

This statement will change the text property on the textbox at runtime. This property is "**text**".

An example of a button and its textual property is set with "**content.**"

butMy1.content="ABCDE"

Content will change a button's visible property.

Conditionals

I will just talk about what we are using, although conditionals are universal in most programming languages.
You will see =, <,> and <> used here as a conditional decision which usually determines the direction of the conditional operation.

If Then Else

If Then Else is used a lot in our code. If a condition is met, then do something. If a condition is not equal, then do something else. Setting a variable is usually the thing that is done, but the whole code flow can be changed by calling a subroutine.

```
If a="123" then
   LiteOn=true
elseif a="567" then
   LIteOn=false
else
   LiteOn=True
end If
```

A simple if-then and end-if can be used too

Do While Loop

A do-while-loop is a looping conditional we will use. It will crash your program eventually if you put it into an indefinite loop. This is an excellent place to put a break in debug mode if you are stuck and your code is crashing. Using debug mode and breaks in your code will allow you to find issues quickly.

Here is an example of a while loop. You can halt the loop by using **end do** or the conditional looking for an x value will end it at 8. LiteOff is a Boolean an. If it is false, the code will exit the do loop.

```
dim x as integer=0
do
   If LiteOff=false then
      exit do
   End if
   x=x+1
while x<8
```

For Next

For...next is typically used in a counting conditional where you need to move up and down a string or something else.

```
Dim x as integer =0
For x=1 to 25
        'x would increase its count
Next x
```

Or

```
Dim ns as string=""
Dim s as string="ABCDE FEGD 123"
For x=1 to astringlenght
        If mid(s,1,x)<>" " then
          ns=mid(s,1,x) & ns        ' concatenates existing ns
        ElseIf mid(s,1,x)="."
          Exit for
                                ' Exists
        End if
Next x
```

ns should be the new string with no spaces.

Events

Events are used in event handling. This is how we can make changes when something happens. Each object usually has an interrupt, or at least the ones we are working with typically do. Typically, events are a subroutine or function. They are typical methods of a button or textbox triggered or raised as events.

There are many kinds of events with each of these objects that can be used. What we use most are the textbox and button events. For the timer event, we must manually add an event for the timer based on a timing interval, since it is not a GUI control and it is triggered by time. It is an object where we add an interrupt.

Note: A lot of the code examples are text wrapped. For instance, butgetdata_click should be on the same line with the Private Sub…. Throughout this book, this will be common. I tried to reduce the size to allow most code lines to be shown on one line throughout, but that is not the case all the time.

```
Private Sub butgetdata_Click(sender As Object, e As RoutedEventArgs) Handles
butgetdata.Click

     'something would happen on the _click event
End Sub
```

There are many other events. You can edit data and do a lot more things in events. Subroutines and Functions are the results of those events. Putting a lot of source code directly inside of a button or any event from our GUI event handlers should be avoided if possible. I have placed the code in some in button and textbox events for ease of understanding in this book.

One reason to separate the code is that when you rename a GUI control, it will cause the event name to be renamed. Creating your own subroutines, and calling those routines in the events usually works best.

Notice below that the timer is setup in the initialize portion of code. You do not need to understand this except to know it is required. An Import statement is always required for the dispatch timer. Public Sub New() is a subroutine you should add at the top of every project. InitializeComponent() is required when you use Public Sub New() to allow normal initialization to occur.

```
Public Sub New()
    InitializeComponent()
    AddHandler mytimer.Tick, AddressOf mytimer_tick  ' Handler Call

End Sub


Private Sub mytimer_tick(ByVal sender As Object, ByVal e As EventArgs)
        'Obviously, things are checked here
End Sub
```

This routine typically is used to show something has changed. A variable's state is checked for a true or false value from an electronic button event or Raspberry Pi GPIO pin state.

Visual Studio IDE Setup

In order to get started with Visual Basic, you need to install the Integrated Development Environment or IDE. Microsoft has a free product called Visual Studio Community 2017, and it includes many languages you may want to along with Visual Basic.

This product will need to be installed, to utilize and program the samples provided in this book. Go to the Visual Studio downloads using a Google search, since it is possible this download page may be moved. The proper place to download the IDE right now is https://www.visualstudio.com/downloads/

Again, you need to download Visual Studio Community 2017, or later. These projects were all done in Microsoft Visual Studio Community 2017, a free IDE. Once Visual Studio is installed, you can setup your environment. We will utilize Visual Basic for all examples.

Note: I highly suggest setting your Pi up initially using an Ethernet cable. I have had some issues with the WI-FI dropping during developmental sessions. Use the hard-line Ethernet to your device, if possible. It is also much faster and easier to setup on your Pi.

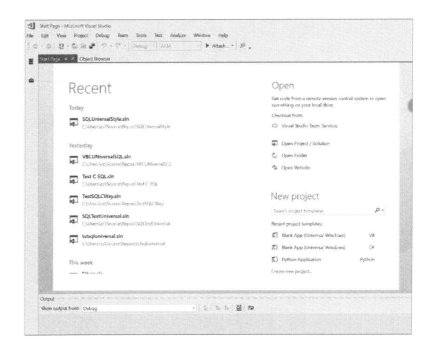

Startup screen for Visual Studio 2017

From here select File and New Project as shown below.

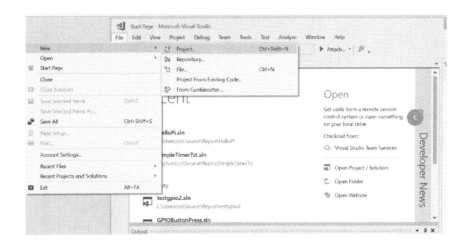

Startup screen shows a selection of a new project.

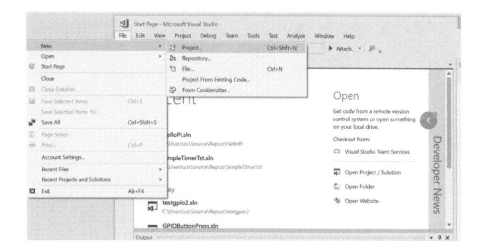

Usual selection of new project shown.

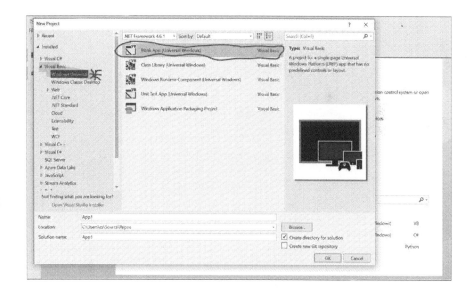

The graphic above shows picking Visual Basic and Blank Universal as your New Project.

This screen will result from your selections. Once Visual Basic/Windows Universal, and Blank App (Universal Windows) are selected. The red outline and notation show those selections. Notice you can change the name of your program. You should be sure you know where the working directory is located. If you are using GitHub (a code repository), you may want a single repository directory per project. I suggest you leave GitHub alone though unless you are very familiar with it.

Selecting **Create | New Git Repository** may also be useful for backing up your application. Remember the Git Repository is a public utility viewable by anyone unless you are paying for it. Github is not required, and I suggest you do not use it initially.

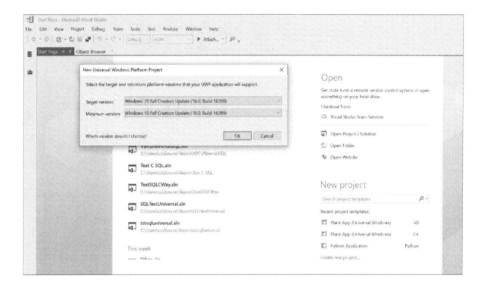

Target and Minimum version selection.

I highly suggest selecting and setting your system up to utilize these latest versions or newer of the Windows 10 Creators Update. The one used for these samples was Build 16299.

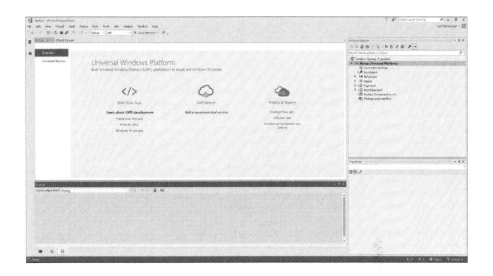

The result of the project creation prior.

The screen you are seeing is visible because nothing else has been chosen from Solution Explorer.

On the next page, I have a more significant representation of the Solutions Explorer window shown at right above. It usually is on the right of the page. If you do not see it, it is selectable in the **File | View | Solution Explorer.**

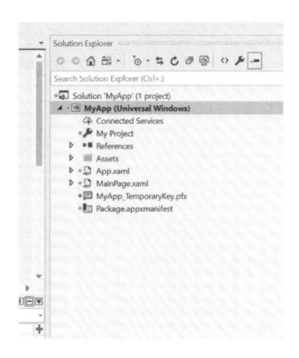

Solution Explorer project window

Note the name of the program is (MyApp). It also says we are using Universal Windows. This Solution explorer looks right, so far.

Note: Xamarin is also run out of Universal, but only in C# and only for Android and IOS. Android Studio has similar XAML Screens and positioning, but it does require Java programming.

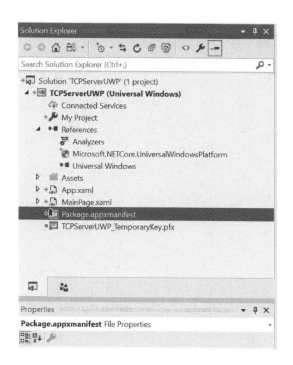

Package appxmanifest is mainly used by us in Splash Screen.

This is another project, called TCPServerUWP. The **References** are the libraries used to do development.
Microsoft.NETCore.UniversalWindowsPlatform and Universal Windows are always included in the references of a new project. The **Assets** area or folder is where you put your Icons for development and other graphics.

MainPage.xaml can be right clicked with your mouse to get to Design or XAML mode, and this is your screen design or GUI.

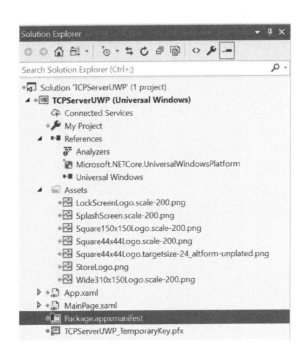

Assets screen on Solution Explorer

I highly suggest you just use the GUI or Design Screen to drag and drop and use the Properties windows at first.

Package.appxmanifest has all the icons, artwork, and graphics used throughout your project. All that we will need to change is the splash screen here if you want it to use one. No Icons or other art requirements necessary.

Once you have selected the MainPage.xaml you will see a screen like the next one showing **Loading Designer.**

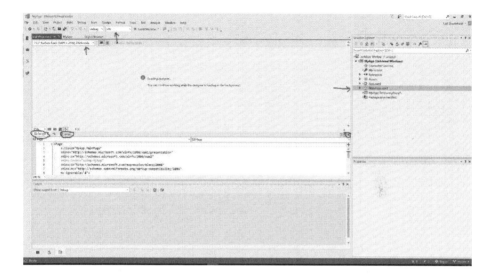

Design windows for your application.

Selecting MainPage.xaml allows toggles between XAML and DESIGN for the application. This is your design window for the GUI design. Usually, the designer can take a few seconds to a minute to build your application, and you may have to rebuild it from time to time.   I have had occasions where I had to switch from ARM to 64 and back to get it to work right on my screen.

The split screen is sometimes helpful. You can edit the XAML window directly and watch your screen change (**Design**) the **XAML** text.   Note the changes in your XAML text as it reflects your selection of properties.

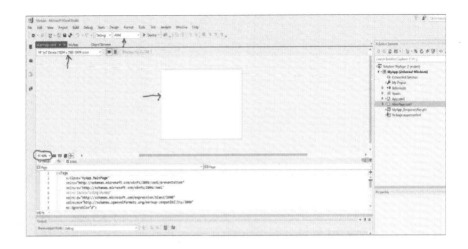

Getting Started with your Project Initial Setup

I put arrows in to show you some setup items for your Visual Studio. These items are crucial to set up when you start. Selecting **10" IoT Device** is not a bad way to go and what I recommend. I use the 7" touch screen recommended by Raspberry Pi Foundation to test, or my 32" monitor. I have settings that have worked well for me that I will share on the 7" screen.

Using this 10" IoT works for me by just by utilizing the left side of the screen or adjusting it for most of these examples. Later you will want to create a screen type precisely like you use to make positioning the GUI that results from XAML design and text. Truthfully, there is not a right answer without knowing your device screen that is being used to test. Play with it in the beginning and refine it for your device with the device resolution settings.

Note: It is best to do all this setup in the beginning and before you start coding.

The resolution of my Pi 7" touchscreen is 800x480, so this is what I will use throughout the text for page and grid settings and page settings. If your display is the same, then I expect you will use that setting. Naturally, I suggest you create your target device and selection for screen resolution if you use it all the time. I will use the grid for examples here since we know the device size is constant. Many types of screens might make sense if various monitors are to be used.

There is a page to be setup along with the grid which will typically be set the same as grid at 800x480. There are numerous screen layouts available like RelativePane, Canvas, ViewBox, and ScrollViewer. Right-click on the grid and those selections will be shown, under **Change Grid Type**. For this book, I will use grid and page that defaults on **10" IoT Device** and again go 800x480 for me. There is documentation to help you if those are areas are something you want to discover later. The documentation is all on the Microsoft site.

Select **ARM** processor. (for the Pi)
NOTE: If you want to test on the Windows machine you are using, you can usually do it. Select 64 and Local to test it locally.

Now you are ready to select a Device in Visual Studio. I suggest using **Remote Machine** at the top. This requires your Remote IoT device be setup correctly. This testing will be live testing, and you can debug your application while running it on your Remote Machine (Raspberry Pi).

The bottom left circle (previous example) shows the percentage view and the arrow just above shows the current display size. Below it shows being set to 100%.

The split screen shows the XAML text and the GUI Design screen together. You can watch the XAML change as you move Buttons and Textboxes on the screen. These items are all changed in the XAML Text.

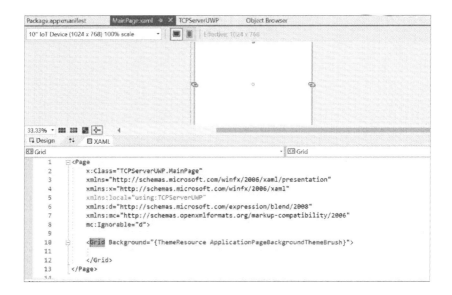

XAML screen and the choices on the left for the device.

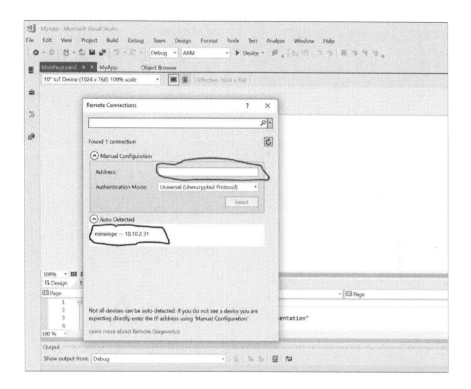

Remote Machine connection selections on Visual Studio Community

Remote Machine is utilized when you want to preview and test the device you are planning to use.

miniwinpc is the standard Raspberry Pi computer name used by default. The Auto Detect will usually find it. If your Pi does not show up, the IP Address can be typed in. Be sure the IP Subnets are the same on the development machine and the Raspberry Pi. In my case, my PC is at 10.10.2.100. The first three group of numbers must be the same Ex: (10.10.2).

Many things can disrupt this connectivity being seen. It must be a device allowed on your network, and parameters must be set to enable your Raspberry Pi device to be seen by your Windows 10 computer. Review the previous sections on preparing your Raspberry Pi for more info.

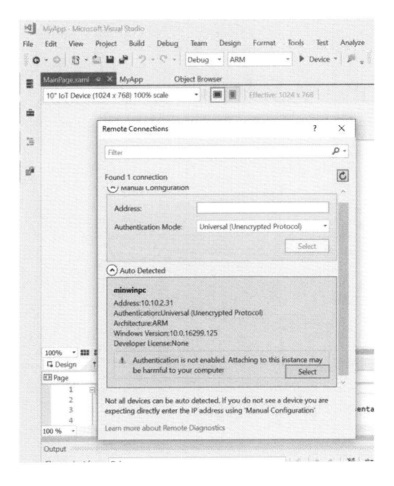

Notice the Warning along with Remote Connection setting.

I do not know a good way around this warning, and it can be ignored to continue. If there is a Developer License required, I am not aware of you needing it at this point.

Now you are ready to begin.

You must be able to get to at least these steps down to begin trying the examples. Start fresh every time with a new Visual Basic Universal project and name your project. Be sure you know where you are saving your projects.

On the default screen or grid, make it fit for you.
1) *Choose New Project in Visual Studio*
2) *Select Visual Basic Universal under Visual Basic*
3) *Name it **HelloPi2** or as the name of the project.*

The resulting screen from the actions above.

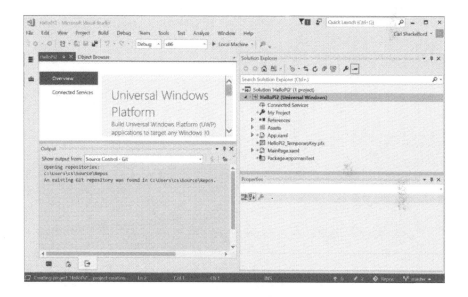

Screen From 1,2,3

Selecting the GUI or XAML Design file MainPage.xaml you will get **Loading Designer**... After a few seconds, the screen setup will probably default to **13.5 Surface Book**.

For our purposes, we will change this to **10" IoT Device**. I use 800 width and 480 height for the grid and page, but you may have different resolutions depending on your monitor.

Note: You will tire hearing me use this resolution, please use yours. It is only right for the monitor I have.

Before compiling and running the application, we must setup the processor type and tell the compiler where we which device or what kind of emulation we are using.

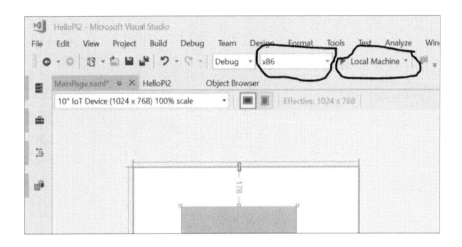

Processor Type and Emulator on Local Machine or Remote Machine.

I circled the places we need to change the processor and display machine. Set processor selection that defaults to **x86** to **ARM**. This marking is visible and circled in the previous screen.
I like to test on my Pi device when using IoT. The best way to do that is setup a Remote Machine on the button.

I do not have my Raspberry Pi connected or turned on as a Windows IoT device. I will show you what you will see if no connection is available your network.

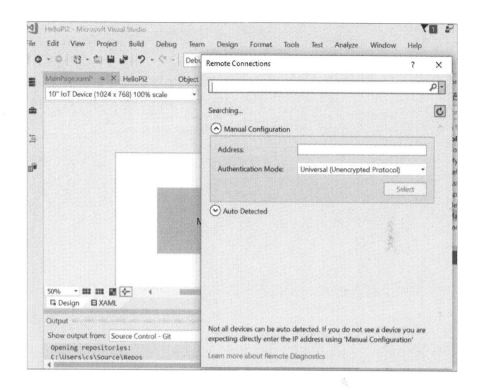

Selecting Remote Machine with None Available

Initially, you may put your address which is shown in your Windows 10 IoT OS on the Pi. The Remote Machine selection will typically detect your device, if not type the address in Address box ex: (10.10.2.31 for me).

Once selected, the screen will show **Remote Machine** like below.

Remote Machine is selected to show Debug info and use your device.

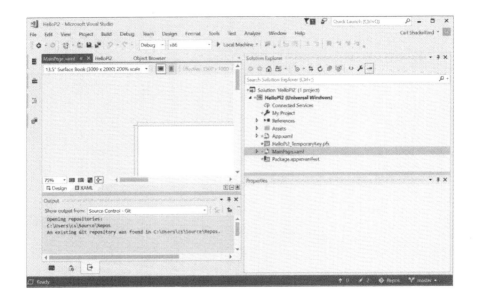

Screen after MainPage.xaml is double-clicked.

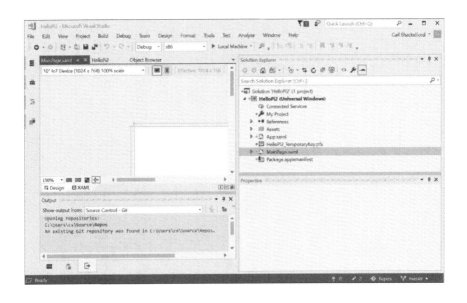

Screen After the Device Screen was changed to 10" IoT device

Set your Grid name on the white background screen in properties to the right. Set width 800 by width 480 for both the grid and page by clicking on the grid and using the properties of the grid. If there is an outside page then clicking to the right of it and selecting the page and adjust the sizes.

Adjust your Windows so you can see your tools and Windows. Most Solid lines have handles and allow for Windows to adjusted.

Eventually, by changing to 50% view and moving the Output down and the Solutions Explorer to the right, you have the screen below. You will need to set the width and height in the Properties window below after clicking on the screen.

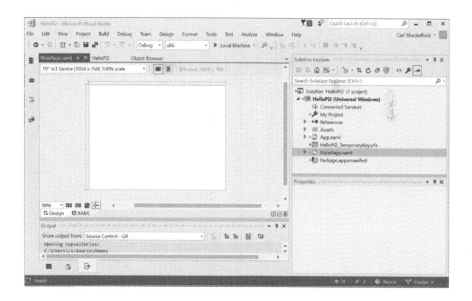

Resulting Windows by adjusting everything and not using 800x480.

On the left of the screen is a Toolbox.

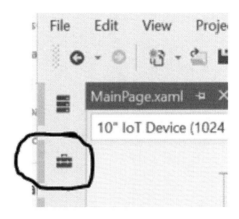

Toolbox to put controls on the Grid

From this toolbox click and the resulting popup, we will select a **Button**.

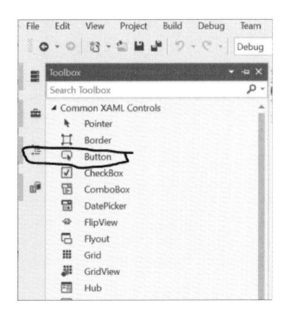

Button From Toolbox

Hold your mouse button and drop or drag it on the screen.

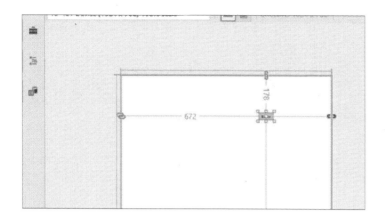

GUI (Design Screen) shown adding a button from the toolbar.

Grab the handles of the Button control) stipulated by small squares on the right or left corner and make it bigger or smaller. The grid is set so changing it here will change the Width and Height of the grid.

We are not creating a project yet just learning to move around in Visual Studio.

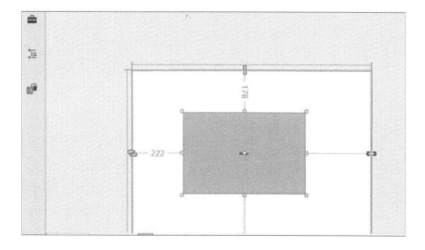

The Button control is shown expanding by grabbing the handles.

After this adjusted, we will set a few properties in the properties window on the right.

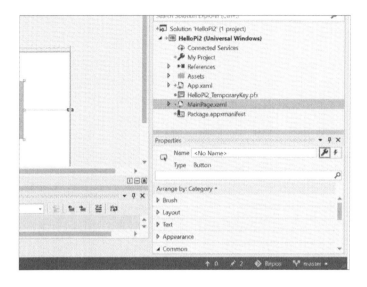

The Screen showing the Properties windows for the Button Control

The screen for Properties usually is on the right under Solutions Explorer shown above.

Click on > **Text** and change the font to 45 px, and set it to Bold

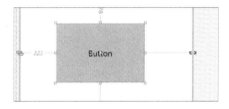

The button on Design Grid

Set the **Content** below in the properties of the Button Control to **MYPI**.
Change the Name above to ButMyPi

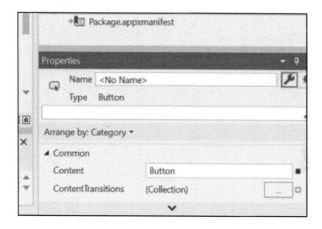

Properties Window for Button.

The **Properties** Windows should look like this. And the properties Name
and Content should look like the next screen.

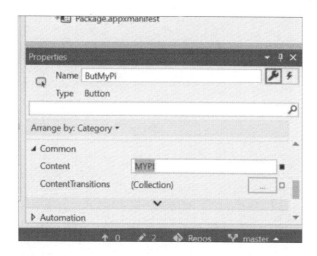

*The Properties Screen for a **Button** Control and setting Context.*

Your resulting screen should look like this.

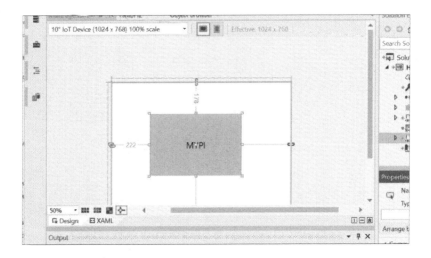

Design screen on the Visual Studio - Visual Basic IDE

A little overkill for walking you through properties, but this is a simple way to show something on the screen and get you started.

Note: The property most used of Textbox is "text" and not "content" like the Button. This is what is shown on that control on the GUI or Screen.

Note: Your XAML and Design screens are there, and you can split them on the screen. I circled the icon that is also helpful for toggling XAML and Design.

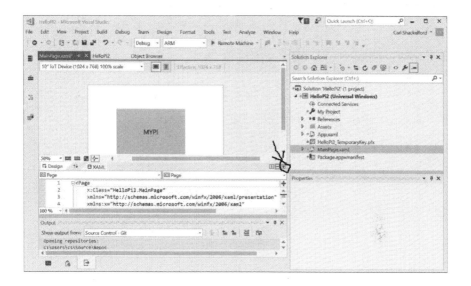

Visual Basic MainPage.XAML design screen & resulting XAML text

Now Select **Remote Machine** to compile and load to your Raspberry Pi Windows IoT device. Debug is also selected beside ARM.

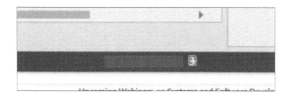

Output activity when using Remote Machine

At the bottom of the development screen during compilation, the output screen at the bottom right will show you the activity.

The following information was due to an error I received. I thought it might be good to take you through it and resolve it. If you did not get an error, then move forward and ignore this.

Start of the Error and resolution (if you want to follow it)
Got to the bottom left

Selecting Error:
I got a DE6957: Failed to connect to the device. This meant the network was not connected when it tried to deliver code and setup to my Pi.

Note: Use an Ethernet cable if possible when testing. WI-FI works fine but is more susceptible to issues than a hard line.

*Bottom screen after Clicking **x 1 Error***

Errors will appear at the bottom left of the page if you have not changed your views. You need to understand errors. You will get a few of these, but it is easy to see what happened and fix it.

The IDE recorded my **Remote Machine** settings, but it closed before I saw I had mistyped the IP address. I right clicked the HelloPi2 (Universal Windows) properties and selected Properties, and Debug shows your device.

There are other paths to fix this. It is in the Project Properties accessible by right-clicking on the name beside (Universal Windows) in the Solution Explorer window shown below.

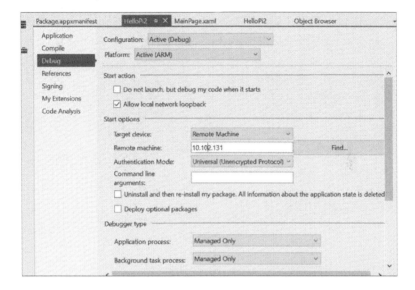

Remote screen setup for TCP IP Address

Obviously, 10.10.2.131 was incorrectly typed. This was corrected (10.10.2.13) as it should have happened the first time and found. Selecting **Remote Machine** restarted the compile and delivery.

End of Error Resolution

BACK ON TRACK.

Select MainPage.xaml

Design at the top and clicking on Remote Machine.

It usually takes a minute or two to upload everything if you are loading to your Raspberry Pi as a Remotely Machine. You must be patient. There are many areas and icons at the bottom of the screen to review during the process. Direct wired Ethernet makes your Raspberry Pi much faster during code transfers.

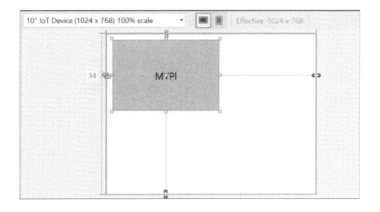

MyPi Button moved to the left of the screen.

I adjusted this to the left-hand corner since my screen is 7" and this emulator design is 10". On Grid, I set the properties 800x480. You may have to reset margins to 0 if they are not set that way.

Adjust the percentage in the bottom left for your design grid which is the view you will see.

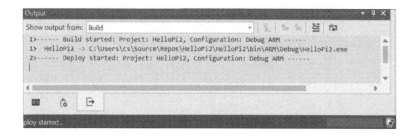

*Bottom left output screen during building and deploying to a **Remote Machine** or any build process.*

Status screen from Output while compiling and deploying. Expect a splash screen first and then your screen.

Default Splash Screen image from this project

This can be changed in Package.appxmanifest. You can change this graphic and should for anything you plan to release. There is a lot of documentation about this on Microsoft's site. There is also a startup ICON. For the Pi, the splash screen is all that you need or really can see. The X and Box are the graphic centered.

Same Project with device and x64

*Note: You could use **Device** and **x64** to test. This is how Universal and Visual Basic looks for this exercise on your Windows 10 development screen. In most cases, the GUI and layout can be tested here by changing from **ARM** to x64 and **Remote Machine** to **Device**. Testing the GPIO or electronics on regular Windows is not possible without some type of emulation library for the Raspberry Pi loaded.*

Now you have a full description of how to start up a project. A similar process will need to be followed for each project.

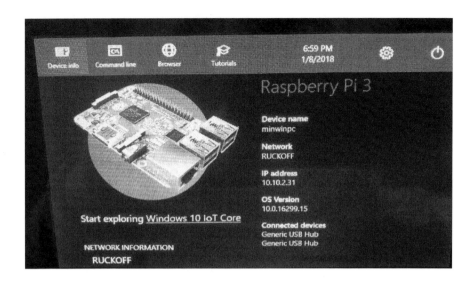

My Raspberry Pi IoT prior to upload.

There are a lot of steps to getting a project setup when you have to include each step. The process is not that hard though once you do a few projects. I segued into a real error because that is where it usually is crucial to have help. I will give you problems like this as they happen to me. I have written code many years and still will have an error from time to time.

Visual Basic Projects

We are finally ready to code! This is the main reason we started this journey, so we could use Visual Basic for our code. Some of the basics have been shown prior, to get everything setup and running.

On the first project, I will review some of those things and take you step by step through the sample code. **HiPi** is a typical Hello World type of application much like all the languages taught as a first project.

HelloPiByePi will add a few more controls and show you an If-Then statement. I do not plan to teach you Visual Basic code, except for a few concepts that you can build on. There is a world of examples on the internet about conditional statements, and I am sure most of you already know the basics.

I wanted to include an example or two about timing and using a timer. I think these will help you down the road. These are in the next few chapters.

At this point. I wanted to show you the GPIO, another cool capability of the Pi. GPIO is the heart of robotics and all electronics. A simple example will illustrate Visual Basic is more than capable of managing complicated code and creating electronic results. Once you have the GPIO working, there is a myriad of things you can create.

File operations are a standard function of most operating systems. I felt you needed an introduction and at least one way to read and write to a file. Configuration, logging, data collection, and many more things are done this way. You might even put a registration code to allow someone to use your program, and use an algorithm to get an official Serial number from a MAC Address.

I also wanted to show you that many more things can be done such as collecting data outside your limited environment. Not only can you have a database on the microSD Chip, but you can have a SQL Server or MySQL or even an Oracle database that you can access. Albeit that it should be a JSON or SOAP process used here. The direct SQL Server access method it is acceptable in some situations. This application accesses a database on WInHost which is a Microsoft SQL Server database.

I do not recommend this method for secure data unless it is more secure across the internet. For around $100 a year, you can get 2-3 Gigs of SQL Server storage accessible from a hosting provider. All you need is a Wi-Fi connection in most cases. You can do things like adding a barcode scanner, collect manufacturing inventory data, or enter contacts in a CRM system. In-house, or with the appropriate security this way of accessing SQL Server can be used,

This setup could be in manufacturing and be a data collection station. I know a significant manufacturer of automobiles in the US that has the Pi on their assembly lines in different capacities.

HelloPi

Program Name:

HelloPi

Purpose:

An introduction to creating a project and program as your first Hello World type application on Windows 10 IoT for the Pi.

Tools Needed:

Basic Pi Computer.

Skills Gained:

Introduction to setting up a GUI-Graphic User Interface (setup screen) and having something appear on the screen you created.

Importance:

This is your beginning to learning GUI's and controls. It is a lot to digest in the beginning. This is just to get you started, and it will get easier. This is the is the basic of programming Visual Basic our Hello World.

Description:

This project will be like the Hello, World! programs you may have seen in other languages. The only difference is it will appear on your Pi since we are sending and testing everything on our device.

I will go into more detail on this first one to be sure you get the steps, so here we go.

Start-Up you Visual Studio Community 2017 or newer.

Go to >**File** | **New** | **Project**

On the New Project window.

Choose **Visual Basic |Windows Universal** and below beside **Name:**
Change it from the default to **HelloPi** and take notice where you
Location/Folder is that it is being stored in.

Select the <**OK**> button.

Be sure The Target and Minimum versions are the latest Creators Update
16299 is the one used here.

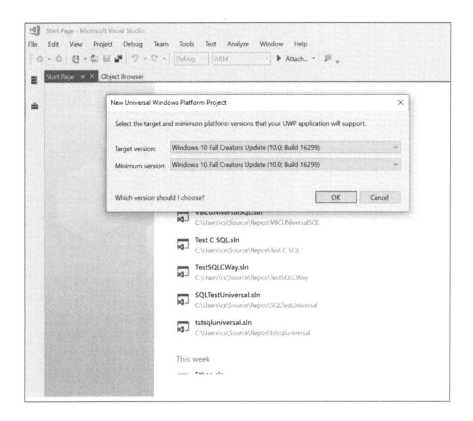

Screen setting up programming environment shown previously.

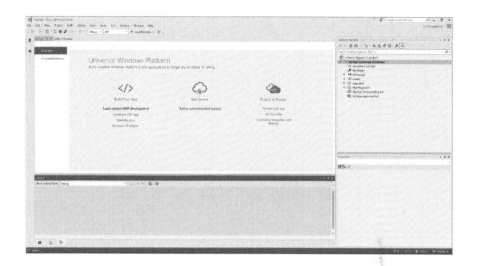

This is the initial screen you will see once the project is built.

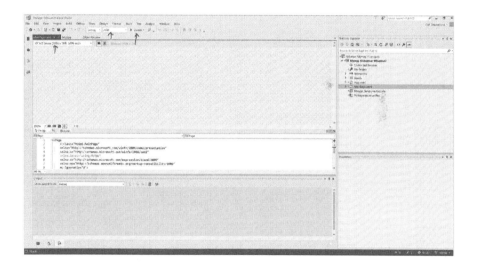

This has the XAML text viewable and can easily be toggled for the GUI view.

Fix the Machine above by changing it from **x86** the default to **ARM**. Be Sure your Pi is setup and reachable from your computer. Set **Device** to **Remote Machine**, so we can use our real device for testing. Your Pi computer needs to be turned on and on the network.

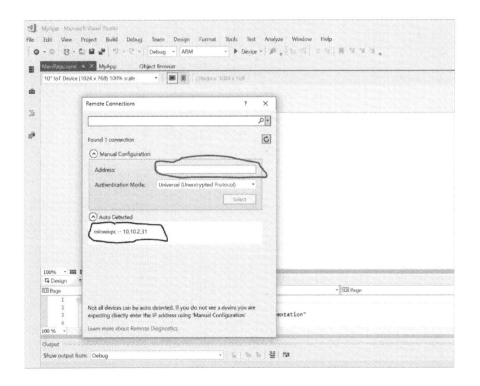

Remote Machine Setup screen.

In the **Remote Connections** window, your device should appear if it is online. If you do not see your device, continue and try the **Auto Detected** button.

Get the IP Address of your Pi from the System info screen of your Raspberry Pi and type it in **Address:** in the textbox, then click select.

Click on MainPage.xaml under Solution Explorer on the right.
It will appear as a selection in a tab on the top with a screen and usually will say **13.5 Surface Book** as a default.   The viewable size is in the left corner as a percentage. On my machine, the default screen size is 13.65%. Every IDE environment is different as is your screen resolution

and size, so find something easy to work with your device. I will use the 50% view for my screen.

Adjust the Grid and page size to 800x480. This is best set prior to development and set margins to 0 also in the Grid. Use what your screen needs, and experiment until you find what your standard setup should be.

Selecting the white or grid area will reveal those properties on the bottom right side under **Properties.**

You can take the handles of the different screen objects and move them out of your way. This finished a repeat of the setup instructions.

Let's build the project.

You should have a Toolbox on the left like the one below.

*This shows the **Toolbox** is available on the left.*

Using Textbox, and select it to be used on your Pi Screen. For this one, click on the toolbox and drag it to the screen. It should look like the screen below now.

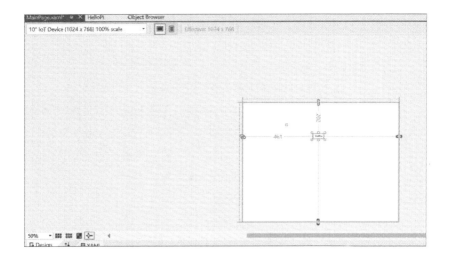

The Designer IDE after dragging a button control onto it.

Now we can adjust this grid.

Since I have a 7-inch screen, I will adjust it to the top left of this screen. If you know the resolution of your screen, you can set it up here.

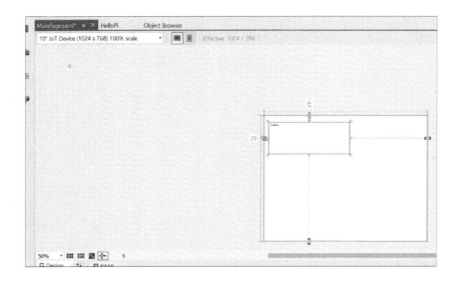

The Designer screen on the Visual Studio IDE

Now it's time to set some properties of the control/object. We are going to want it to be bigger and centered. You should always name your objects too, so you can refer to them in code later.

Select your newly created button and go to Properties on the right-hand bottom corner. You can see the properties of the Textbox. I have a picture of what this looks like on the next page.

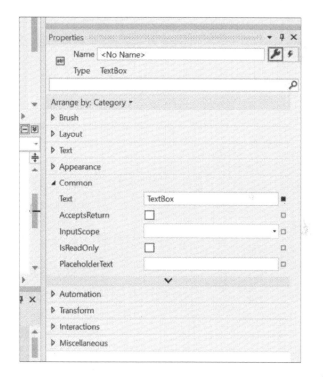

Properties of Textbox above from the left part of the screen

1. Textbox
   a. Name = **txthello**
   b. Text = **HELLO PI**

You will see the change immediately

I am showing you below in the property windows how to change the point size next to the Font name.

Change Text Point Size to 48 px by >Text **48 px**

Change Alignment to Center by Selecting the Paragraph symbol circled below

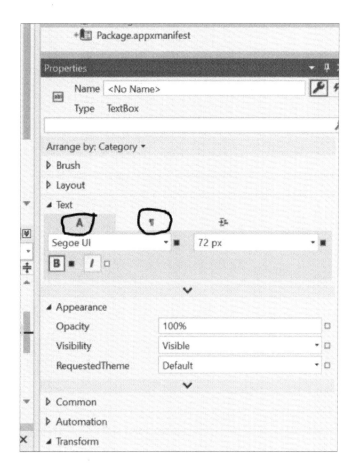

Properties screen showing Alignment and Font info for the textbox

92

The following Screen will appear once you have set **Center** for the alignment of the Textbox. This next screen will show you these property settings in the properties window. The properties are not as easy as standard Visual Basic, but they are user-friendly enough.

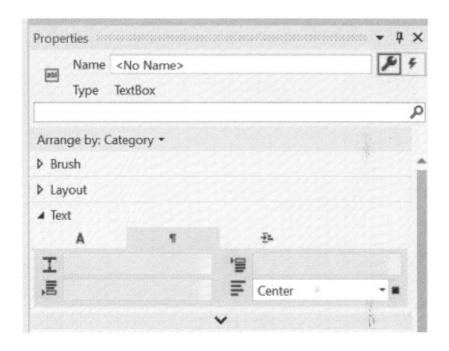

Properties to set center on the Textbox

You should always name a textbox with "txt" prefix and a name this txtHelloPi. To change the runtime value in code, you will use the runtime code txthelloPi.text="Hello Pi".

For multiple lines on a Textbox control, there is a Wrap property. It was called multiLine for textbox in other Visual Studio products.

You have two primary controls for textboxes. The textblock is typically used for read-only or labels where lines are not used. Lines can be added. For my purposes, unless it is a label, I will use a Textbox control.

Textblock automatically wraps text where Textbox must have the Wrap set.

The resulting MainPage.xaml Design should be shown next.

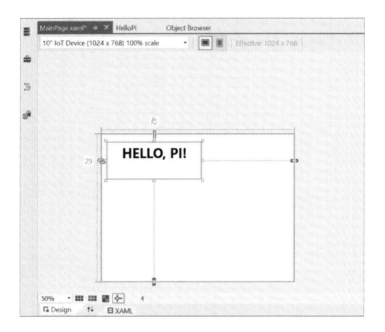

Design screen or Grid.

The property screen should look like the following image.

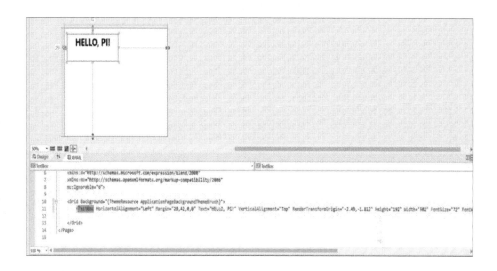

Notice the XAML code that is created above.

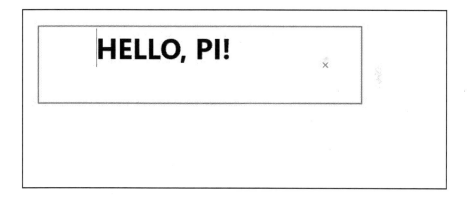

This is the GUI or Screen as it should look.

Do not be too concerned about locations of controls, let's just get this working on the screen.

This is how GUI or Screen setups will be given to you in the future.

1. Create textbox
   a. Name=txthellopi

b. Font layout=center

c. Text="**HELLO, PI!**

2. Setup Grid

a. Name=myGrid

b. Width=800

c. Height=480

It is simple creating the screen, but I just wanted to show you everything you set up is updated in the XAML text. You can manually adjust things there too.

This is the way the code should look for the MainPage.xaml from the designer shown in the next graphic. This code line wrapped due to limited size on this page. The text can be edited in the XAML Design area, but be careful. ALWAYS make changes in XAML before you start coding, so a restart would not be as painful.

```
<Page
  x:Class="HelloPi.MainPage"
  xmlns="http://schemas.microsoft.com/winfx/2006/xaml/presentation"
  xmlns:x="http://schemas.microsoft.com/winfx/2006/xaml"
  xmlns:local="using:HelloPi"
  xmlns:d="http://schemas.microsoft.com/expression/blend/2008"
  xmlns:mc="http://schemas.openxmlformats.org/markup-compatibility/2006"
  mc:Ignorable="d" Width="800" Height="480">

  <Grid x:Name="mygrid" Background="{ThemeResource
ApplicationPageBackgroundThemeBrush}" Width="800" Height="480">
    <TextBox x:Name="txtboxhellopi" HorizontalAlignment="Left"
Margin="29,42,0,0" Text="HELLO, PI!" VerticalAlignment="Top"
RenderTransformOrigin="-2.49,-1.812" Height="130" Width="554" FontSize="48"
FontWeight="Bold" FontFamily="Segoe UI" TextAlignment="Center"
TextChanged="TextBox_TextChanged"/>
    <TextBox HorizontalAlignment="Left" Height="34" Margin="609,241,0,0"
Text="TextBox" VerticalAlignment="Top" Width="168"/>

  </Grid>
</Page>
```

As I have mentioned, the Width=800 and height=480 may not be right for your equipment. The settings should be whatever your monitor screen resolution is. You should change the default grid and page sizes to meet your environment. Notice it is there twice.

Below is that representation in the XAML highlighted below.

```
<Grid x:Name="mygrid" Background="{ThemeResource
ApplicationPageBackgroundThemeBrush}" Width="800" Height="480">
```

```
' The Blank Page item template is documented at
https://go.microsoft.com/fwlink/?LinkId=402352&clcid=0x409
''' <summary>
''' An empty page that can be used on its own or navigated to within a Frame.
''' </summary>
Public NotInheritable Class MainPage
    Inherits Page

    Private Sub TextBox_TextChanged(sender As Object, e As
TextChangedEventArgs)

    End Sub
End Class
```

This is all the source code that is required to make this work. It is good to have your code structured like this, so you can set specific parameters when your application starts.

You should add the Public Sub New() which must have IntitializeComponent() to allow it to work. This was code that was required in previous versions, must now be added. It is the way you should start your application since it runs first upon startup of the app.

This Sub is shown below.

```
Public Sub New()
    InitializeComponent()
```

```
      'add startup stuff here
End Sub
```

Below I added a variable x that will be seen throughout the Class.
It is shown at the top in the class. Class level variables are global to the whole class.

```
' The Blank Page item template is documented at
https://go.microsoft.com/fwlink/?LinkId=402352&clcid=0x409
''' <summary>
''' An empty page that can be used on its own or navigated to within a Frame.
''' </summary>
' Imports would be above the class
Public NotInheritable Class MainPage
    Inherits Page
    Dim x as string="a"
    Public Sub New()
        InitializeComponent()
        'add startup stuff here
    End Sub
Private Sub TextBox_TextChanged(sender As Object, e As
TextChangedEventArgs)

    End Sub
End Class
```

Ok, let's see if it works now.

Select the green arrow and **Remote Machine** at the top of the page. This should send all the code over to the Pi. This will compile it and deploy it, so be patient. It also puts it in the App area of the Web Device Portal of the Raspberry Pi.

The screen you should see is below on your Pi.

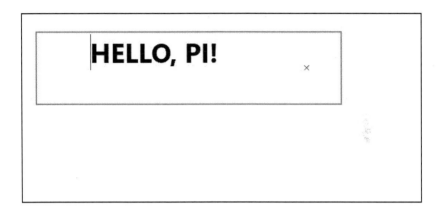

This is the form for the HelloPi program

Note: The Textbox control can be used for many things. It can be used to type in or add and edit data. Textblock can be used for read-only.

Awesome!

You have now written your first Visual Basic program for the Raspberry Pi IoT. Press the red square button at the top to stop the program. Save and exit.

Note: Normally you would have a button, and the event would terminate the code.

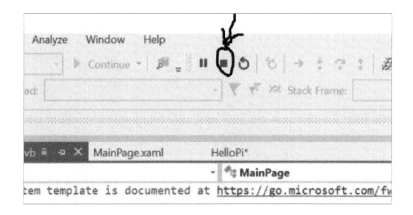

Screen after application as started.

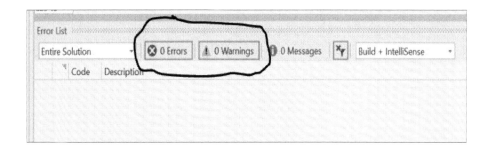

The bottom left of your screen is where Errors and Warning will be displayed.

HelloPiBye

Program Name:

HelloPiBye

Purpose:

To show how to utilize a textblock control and button control to toggle the visual info of the text property in the textblock.

Tools Needed:

Basic Raspberry Pi Computer and connectivity to a monitor, keyboard, power, and your network.

Skills Gained:

This will create a deeper understanding of how to setup a GUI-Graphic User Interface (setup screen) and causing something to appear on the screen.

Importance:

Learning about GUI's and the button and textbox controls.

Description:

This project will bring you into the event handler part of Visual Basic and the Pi. It will also show you how a subroutine can work.

Let's get started. I will allow you to set your environment settings this time.

Create a new project and do everything, name it **HelloPiBye,** and follow the guide for setting up the environment.

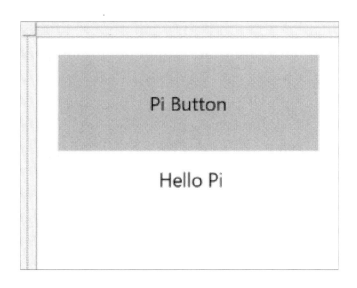

Program design screen.

Your screen something like this. The properties settings and steps to setup your screen are below.

1) Grid (After screen size is chosen)
   a. Name=myGrid

      (If using a 7" Touch PI Screen)
   b. Width=800
   c. Height=480
   d. Set the Page the same if necessary.
2) Create a Textblock and
   a. name= txtinfo
   b. Text= **Hello Pi**
   c. Font=48 px
   d. Size it and move it to the left side of your screen (sizing will be done in future)
   e. Font = Center
3) Create a Button
   a. Content =**Pi Button**

b.   Name=butPi

c.   Set the Font points to 48 or so

Now adjust on your screen. I will show you a copy of my properties window in the next few screenshots.

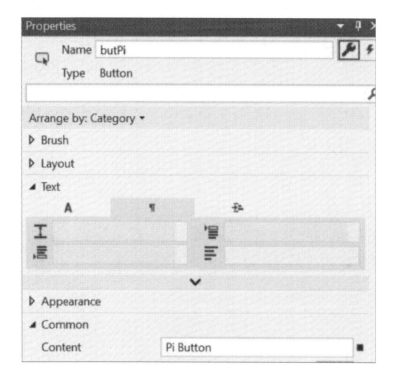

The Button properties setup.

The Textblock Properties are below

Properties after clicking Textblock to Set it to Hello Pi to start

I am sure you got it close. This is all again in the XAML textual presentation too. You should see it on the Design screen.

Now we will setup an event on Button Click or butPi as we renamed it. This is the object name we will refer to with a conditional "If ...then" statement.

Note: A part of the code in the gray areas (') is used to denote comments. I will put comments besides, above, and below code to further describe something. This is just a comment for Visual Basic in the code.

Double-click the button control you created, and it will cause the event to open to allow you to write code.

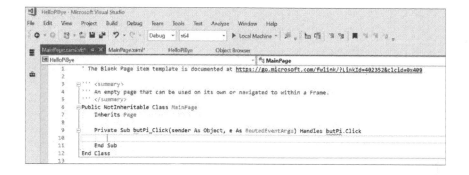

MainPagexaml.vb screen where the code for ButPi control events.

Clicking on the button will show this screen and allow you to edit your source code there. This code below is the same code as above. It just has its text wrapped at the end of the line.

Private Sub butPi_Click(sender As Object, e As RoutedEventArgs) Handles butPi.Click

End Sub

Note: The full syntax you are working on is inside a class on the MainPage.xaml. This object is Inherited to get you going. Do not worry if this is a bit too much information, too soon. I do not plan to take you deep into Object-oriented programming in this book.

Public NotInheritable Class MainPage
    Inherits Page

 Private Sub butPi_Click(sender As Object, e As RoutedEventArgs) Handles butPi.Click

 End Sub
End Class

Just know that you can easily mess up your code by changing things in other areas. Move slowly and carefully at first. Starting over is sometimes better than trying to fix code issues when you are getting started with Visual Basic Universal. Start a new project, if you need to.

Now we are ready to setup a conditional, the "If..Then" statement. Most programs have conditionals statements, and this is the one we will use to toggle information in the Textblock.

We will setup a condition to validate what is in the textblock control we named txtinfo, and rename it's .text property accordingly.
If it is **Bye, Pi!** It will change to **Hello Pi!** And vice versa.
Below is showing how this code is done structured.

```
If txtinfo.text = "Bye, Pi!" Then     ' A conditional
    txtinfo.text = "Hello Pi!"        ' A Change to the Text
  Else
    txtinfo.text = "Bye, Pi!"         ' A Change to the Text
End If
```

Pushing the Pi Button will toggle the value in the textBlock as shown below.

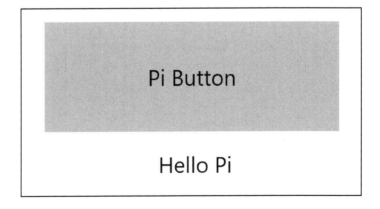

Final Output screen - Pi Button toggles the Hello Pi TextBlock.

Your screen will change by pushing the Pi Button. The textblock will toggle the text property from **Hello Pi** to **Bye, Pi**

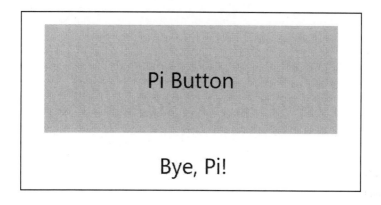

The output screen from the program and Toggle to Bye, Pi!

This is an example using these two controls.

This is an excellent time to at least show you some other features of Visual Basic. It is sometimes easier to test in **x64,** and on your local machine before moving it to the Pi for testing your GUI look and feel as a **Remote Device** on **Arm**.

With no Raspberry Pi GPIO used, the Universal IoT code is usually close enough to test in normal Windows Universal. Just set **x64** and usually, your code will run just fine. The **x64** mode can be done or using **ARM** mode. This mode might make your programming and debugging easier.

*The Toolbar where you can use **x64** on GUI, **ARM** for Remote Machine.*

Another thing to keep in mind is that you can debug or test your code on the Pi while in ARM and Debug using **Remote Machine**. By clicking to the left of your line in the left margin, you can set breakpoints (represented by Red Dots on the margin). This will make your code pause, so you can check variable values and many other things. This will be done in ARM mode and Debug.

The following graphic is an example of **Debug** mode, and the Red Dot in the left margin is a breakpoint. This is extremely helpful if you are working with a sophisticated program.

Using a breakpoint in your program by the button click event will cause it to pause there. You can do many things in the output window and other areas to review different states of variables during your code execution. Using the **Continue** at the top of the page or Step into will continue your code from the pause while in the debug process. The Continue mentioned returns code execution until the next break is hit.

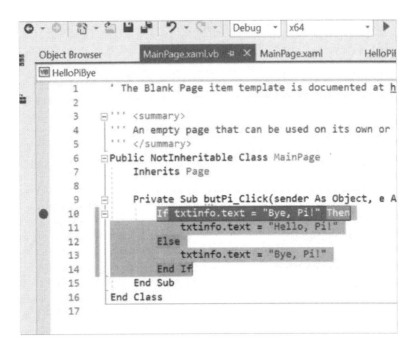

Code window of the finished product.

You have learned enough of the initial code to do a lot of things that can be of use programming your Pi. You can start and stop using conditionals and make changes to controls accordingly. We will build on this in the next application.

SimpleTimer

Program Name:

SimpleTimer

Purpose:

This will show you how to use a timer, progress control, textblock, and event handlers in more detail.

Tools Needed:

Basic Pi Computer.

Skills Gained:

The skill you will learn is how to manage a dispatch timer object interrupt. You will also understand button interrupts(events) better.

Importance:

This timer is used for a lot of projects. Time is a crucial part of programming.

Description:

This project will take you into even more controls and events and handlers. There is a routine for formatting time as well.

Create a new project and name it **SimpleTimer.** Follow the previous instructions for setting up the environment.

This is a timer project that will show you how to setup a timer and check for interrupts/requests to stop or halt the timer. We will talk about pressing a button control and setting a Boolean to false and true. The Timer event controls the timer. A mouse-click or touch on the screen on the button sets everything in motion.

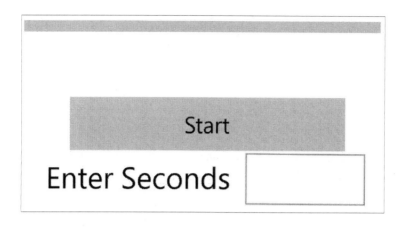

Initial Timer screen at startup.

To operate the timer, you type in seconds in at **Enter Seconds.** You can press **Start** in the application to start the timer. The progress bar at the top will begin with a value of 1. It will count until it reaches the seconds requested or the user can hit **Start** to stop the count where it is.

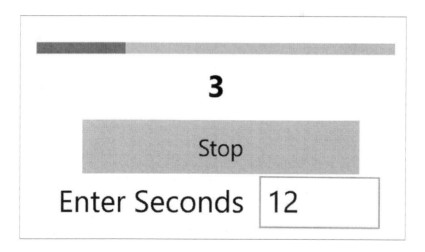

Seconds timer after Time is set and started. This one was stopped at 3 but was setup for 12 seconds.

We will introduce the progress bar shown at the top at 3/12 blue for the progress to 12.   Also, at the bottom of the code, there is a gift. A method for changing the format for converting 60 seconds to 1 minute using the mod function is introduced.   Converting seconds to minutes would be more user-friendly.

There are many new concepts introduced, but the main one is the **dispatch timer** object. The timer format code I have here is not used here, but in other projects, it can be.

Let's start with the project.

Create a new project naming it **SimpleTimer**.

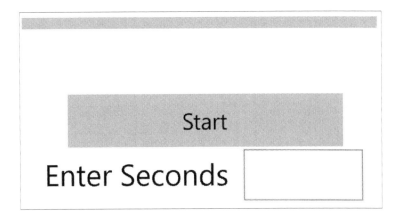

GUI Screen setup in IDE

Set the screens GUI as above, by utilizing the properties below.

Note: Positioning is not crucial to this project, but I will show you some tidbits on that subject.

1. Grid

      a.   Name=MyGrid

      b.   Width=800

      c.   Height=480

      d.   Page should be the same 800x480

4. Setup a Progress Control

      a.   Name= proBar

      b.   Center at the top of the screen

5. Setup a textblock

      a.   Name= txttimer

      b.   Fontsize=48 px (or smaller)

      c.   Set the size of the screen to fit your visible screen

On your button, you can Set the use **HorizontalAlignment** as **Center** margins for horizontal are on top and vertical on the bottom. The next graphic shows the **HorizontalAlignment**. You might need to remove Margins, or set them to 0. This 0 margin setting is set for the top two settings beside **Margin** normally.

Note: Using center sets left and right margin and vertical sets the bottom distance from top and bottom. This can be used. It might help depending on your environment. Other settings for your screen or monitor are available as are different screen types in UWP.

Properties for the txttimer

I usually just drag controls to the position and utilize the **Format** and **Align** to adjust alignment. I wanted you to know this feature is under the objects **Layout** properties.

Ignore the width on the textblock above, this was during testing on x64, and the system changed the width.

Note: Using x64 also can change the width and height of the grid. You may need to change some settings back to fit your Arm processor.

This is enough about positioning. Let us focus on the rest of the controls; I am sure you will be able to set this up without much trouble.

1) Setup a Button
   a. Content=Start
2) Setup a txtblock (a label)
   a. text=Enter Seconds
   b. Font =48 px or appropriate to your screen
   c. name=lblEnterSeconds
3) Setup a textbox
   a. name=txtSeconds
   b. font=48 px same as above
   c. Font position=center

XAML text code should be like below. If you have issues, the text below can be copied into XAML. You should start a new project for this to work well, and setup the screen using this information. We will again set everything to work with a 7-inch display. Be sure your naming is the same for the screen objects.

```
<Page
  x:Class="SimpleTimerTst.MainPage"
  xmlns="http://schemas.microsoft.com/winfx/2006/xaml/presentation"
  xmlns:x="http://schemas.microsoft.com/winfx/2006/xaml"
  xmlns:local="using:SimpleTimerTst"
  xmlns:d="http://schemas.microsoft.com/expression/blend/2008"
  xmlns:mc="http://schemas.openxmlformats.org/markup-compatibility/2006"
  mc:Ignorable="d" Width="800" Height="480">

  <Grid x:Name="MyGrid" Background="{ThemeResource
ApplicationPageBackgroundThemeBrush}" Width="800" Height="480">
    <TextBlock x:Name="txttimer" HorizontalAlignment="Stretch" Height="79"
Text="" TextWrapping="Wrap" VerticalAlignment="Top" Width="548"
FontSize="48" TextAlignment="Center" FontWeight="Bold"
Margin="126,44,126,0"/>
```

```
    <Button x:Name="butstart" Content="Start" HorizontalAlignment="Left"
Height="84" Margin="200,129,0,0" VerticalAlignment="Top" Width="446"
FontSize="36"/>
    <TextBox x:Name="txtseconds" HorizontalAlignment="Left" Height="81"
Margin="485,217,0,0" Text="" VerticalAlignment="Top" Width="194"
InputScope="Number" FontSize="48" RenderTransformOrigin="0.5,0.5"
UseLayoutRounding="False" d:LayoutRounding="Auto">
      <TextBox.RenderTransform>
        <CompositeTransform SkewY="0.244" TranslateY="0.496"/>
      </TextBox.RenderTransform>
    </TextBox>
    <TextBlock x:Name="lblenterseconds" HorizontalAlignment="Left"
Height="73" Margin="161,222,0,0" Text="Enter Seconds" TextWrapping="Wrap"
VerticalAlignment="Top" Width="313" FontSize="48"/>
    <ProgressBar x:Name="probar" HorizontalAlignment="Left" Height="18"
Margin="125,8,0,0" VerticalAlignment="Top" Width="577" Maximum="12"/>

  </Grid>
</Page>
```

Time must be declared by adding a library in an import statement. There are other libraries you can use to control time, but we will use the dispatch timer.

```
Imports Windows.UI
```

must be introduced first.

```
Imports Windows.UI
Public NotInheritable Class MainPage
  Inherits Page
  Public mytimer As New DispatcherTimer
```

I declared the variables at the top of the class to make it easier to share them across the class. This is not necessarily the only way to do this, but I thought it would be clearer this way.

```
SimpleTimerTst                    MainPage                      mytimer

 9          ''' </summary>
10          Imports Windows.UI
11      Public NotInheritable Class MainPage
12          Inherits Page
13          Public mytimer As New DispatcherTimer
14          Public stopit As Boolean = True
15          Public counter As Double = 0  'Public
16          'SimpleTimer1st is only used to show how to set seconds and stop it
17          '   sound and visuals can be used to show the time is reached
18          '   also GPIO out can be used to turn on lights or do other things
19          Public Sub New()
20              InitializeComponent()
21              AddHandler mytimer.Tick, AddressOf mytimer_tick
22          End Sub
23
24          Private Sub butstart_Click(sender As Object, e As RoutedEventArgs) Handles butstart.Click
25              If txtseconds.text <> "" Then
26                  probar.Value = counter          ' progressbar control was shown to introduce you
```

Actual Code window is shown above.

Once you setup the code and the timer AddHandler mytimer.Tick, you will need to add the subroutine below for mytimer_click. It will not be added automatically.

```
Private Sub mytimer_tick(ByVal sender As Object, ByVal e As EventArgs
End Sub
```

These are the first two subroutines (Sub) you will see in the code.

```
Public Sub New()
    InitializeComponent()
    AddHandler mytimer.Tick, AddressOf mytimer_tick
  End Sub
Private Sub mytimer_tick(ByVal sender As Object, ByVal e As EventArgs
End sub
```

The routine mytimer_tick is where the timer will return during each iteration. Before this is activated, the timer object must be initiated. The sequence for starting the time is below. The iteration of time can be at different numbers all in milliseconds. Note here that it is at 1 second or 1000 milliseconds.

```
mytimer.Interval = TimeSpan.FromMilliseconds(1000)
mytimer.Start()
mytimer.Stop()
```

This effectively stops the mytimer_tick from being used the next time it goes in the subroutine.

I think the conditionals below are understandable.

```
If counter > txtseconds.text Then
    mytimer.Stop()    'Tell clock to pause or halt
    butstart.Content = "Time Reached-Restart?" ' & txtseconds.Text
    stopit = True
    'Add Sound here
End If
```

118

Stopit is a Boolean true or false set by the butstart event.

```
' Below is a conditional checking for an error
' There are many ways to do this but Files and things that can  fail need
' to have something to catch errors
Try
   a = txtseconds.Text
Catch ex As Exception
   'No numeric available so
   txtseconds.Text = "5"  ' if nothing is there we set 5 seconds
   Exit Sub
End Try
```

Note the **Try...Catch...End** error handler can be used with the code above. If a non-numeric entry is added into the txtseconds.text property, an error is raised. The Catch gives you a chance to report the error or catch and fix it.

This can be used in your code for file, GPIO, and other operations to keep it from having a significant error and shutting down.

```
' The Blank Page item template is documented at
https://go.microsoft.com/fwlink/?LinkId=402352&clcid=0x409

''' <summary>
''' An empty page that can be used on its own or navigated to within a Frame.
''' </summary>
'''

''' <summary>
''' An empty page that can be used on its own or navigated to within a Frame.
''' </summary>
Imports Windows.UI
Public NotInheritable Class MainPage
   Inherits Page
   Public mytimer As New DispatcherTimer
   Public stopit As Boolean = True
   Public counter As Double = 0  'Public
   'SimpleTimer1st is only used to show how to set seconds
   ' and stop it
```

```vbnet
' sound and visuals can be used to show the time is reached
' also GPIO out can be used to turn on lights or do other things
Public Sub New()
    InitializeComponent()
    AddHandler mytimer.Tick, AddressOf mytimer_tick
End Sub
Private Sub butstart_Click(sender As Object, e As RoutedEventArgs) Handles
butstart.Click
    If txtseconds.text <> "" Then
        probar.Value = counter
        ' progressbar control was shown to introduce you
        probar.Maximum = txtseconds.Text
    End If
    If stopit = False Then
    ' Checks to see if someone tried to stop this
        stopit = True
        butstart.Content = "Start"
    Else
        'Routine below to allow for interupting timer
        'with boolean stopit=false
        butstart.Content = "Stop"
        counter = 0
        stopit = False  ' stop the timer
        'below starts the timer and sets the amount of
        'time between it 1000 Mili or 1 second
        mytimer.Interval = TimeSpan.FromMilliseconds(1000)
        mytimer.Start()
    End If

End Sub
'Used as a timer to count seconds
'Public mytimer As New DispatcherTimer
'    opens this up as an event And
'    you will have To add the Private Sub mytimer
'    it As I have below
Private Sub mytimer_tick(ByVal sender As Object, ByVal e As EventArgs)
    counter = counter + 1
    Dim a As Long

    'Below is a conditional checking for an error
    ' There are many ways to do this but Files and
    ' things that can fail need
    ' to have something to catch errors
    Try
        a = txtseconds.Text
```

120

```vb
        Catch ex As Exception
            'No numeric available so
            txtseconds.Text = "5"
    ' if nothign is there we set 5 seconds
            Exit Sub
        End Try


        'Use the progress bar named probar and counter
        probar.value = counter

        If counter > txtseconds.text Then
            mytimer.Stop()    'Tell clock to pause or halt
            butstart.Content = "Time Reached-Restart?"
            stopit = True
            'Add Sound here maybe
        End If

        If stopit = False Then
            mytimer.Start()

        'Calling a Function that returns a string not used here
        ' txttimer.Text = formattime()
        ' if you do not want conversion you can just use seconds
            txttimer.Text = counter
        Else
            butstart.Content = "Start"
            mytimer.Stop()
        End If

    End Sub

    Private Function isnumeric(text As String) As Boolean
        Throw New NotImplementedException()
    End Function

' The code below is just for your reference.
Public Function formattime() As String
        'Not used in this but introduced here to return
        ' Minutes and Seconds
        'There are many ways you could do this, but this is one
        Dim mod1 As Double = 0
        Dim whole1 As Double = 0
        Dim mods As String = "A"
        Dim wholes As String = "A"
```

```
'If you can use the Global value Counter to
' determine a preset time.
whole1 = counter \ 60      'whole number left over
mod1 = counter Mod 60       'divisor
mods = mod1.ToString.Trim
'not needed introduced .trim
wholes = whole1.ToString.Trim
'not needed introduced

'keep it 00:00
If wholes.Length < 2 Then
    wholes = "0" & wholes
End If

If mods.Length < 2 Then
    mods = "0" & mods
End If
'returns it to the caller
formattime = wholes & ":" & mods

  End Function
End Class
```

There are a lot of new concepts presented in this section. Once you master these concepts, you can utilize them to do some neat things for your future projects.

File Operations

Program Name:

FileOperations

Purpose:

This project demonstrates how to manage files by read, write, and create file operations.

Tools Needed:

Basic Pi Computer.

Skills Gained:

Reading, writing a file and editing in a textbox.

Importance:

Files are great for multiple things like log files, program parameters, and most anything you can imagine.

Description:

Using the file read and write operations for the Windows 10 IoT has a lot of value. Using a read to do something simple like control setup parameters is possible. You may need an easy way to do a config or "ini" type setup file. You could write to the registry, but reading or writing to a local file is more straightforward.

It also might make a project easier to setup, if all that is needed read and write to a file. The kind of files we will work are just regular text files. The files are just one row at a time each row terminated by a CR/LF or Carriage Return and Line Feed denoting the end of each line. We will read and write from what is called a file using UWP-Universal Windows Program parameters for the Pi and IoT.

This can and does function as a simple file editor.

There must be privileges to write and read and create a file. I have not had an issue with privileges on a local drive on the Raspberry Pi, but you may run into that especially if you decide to write to an external drive. We are only using a local file in this example.

Let's get started.

Create the project and name it **fileOperations**.

Once the project is created, and all properties are set, add the following libraries to manage your files and stream processing.

Imports Windows.Storage
Imports Windows.Storage.Streams
Imports System.IO.Stream

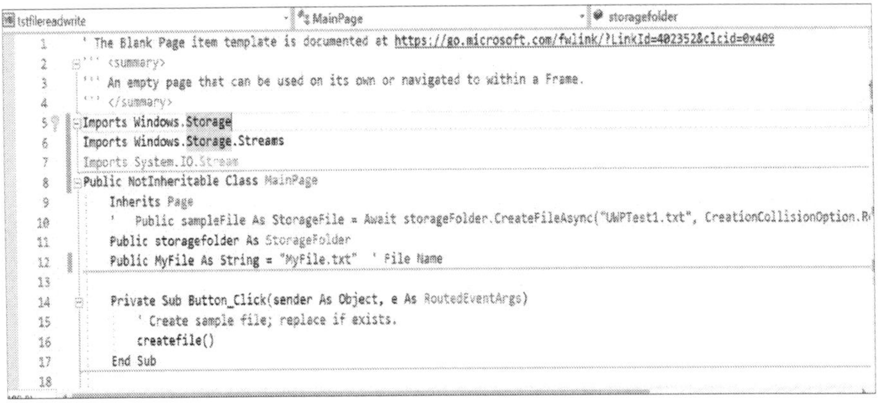

Code windows on my screen

Here is what the GUI looks like on my screen in the next diagram

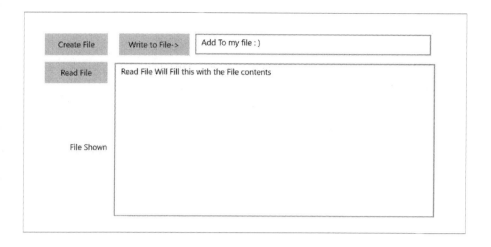

Screen expectations once developed

Ok let's set this up

1. Setup Button Control butCreate
    a. Content=**Create File**
    b. creates a file and deletes the old one
2. Setup Button Control
    a. Name=butWrite
    b. Content=**Write to File**
3. Setup TextBox Control
    a. Name=txtdatain
    b. Text=**Add To My File :)**
4. Setup a Button Control on next line
    a. Name=butRead
    b. Content= **Read File**
5. Setup Textbox Control
    a. Name=txtFilein
    b. Text=**Read File Will Fill this with the file contents**
6. Setup Textblock
    a. Name=?
    b. Text=File Shown

Major Subroutines

ButCreate: creates a new file or deletes and recreates the file there.

ButWrite: writes/appends Write to File-> textbox to the end of the file.

ButRead: reads the complete contents of the file.

There are 2 textbox controls and 3 buttons to perform this project. There are 3 subroutines, and the buttons call those subroutines. Be sure you use the latest creator's editions. Some of these functions might have a different outcome, if old libraries are used.

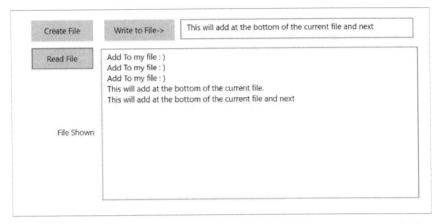

The result of adding some text in the top text box and hitting Read File

The contents of the property txtfile.text are the file contents. Note you can also add data to the textbox (txtdatain.text). It will be appended and saved along with the line of data in the top box. Reading the file (**Read File)** button will show that it was saved.

The textbox has the basic functionality of an editor, as does this application. The textbox control can do a lot in the editing department. We will use only the simplest of features for that control in this project though.

Note: The textbox WRAP property must be on to show multiple lines on the control. Using Textblock Wrap is automatically turned on, but textblock comes with no border lines. Textblock is read-only and is primarily used in Label type situations like the File Shown label.

MyFile.txt is the file name used. The file name could have been created as a variable in an additional textbox property, and it could have been allowed to be changed to create more of an editor. Try this once you get your project working. Try...Catch error handlers should be added around reads, writes, and create activities to report errors.

MainPage.xaml.vb code.

```
' The Blank Page item template is documented at
https://go.microsoft.com/fwlink/?LinkId=402352&clcid=0x409
''' <summary>
''' An empty page that can be used on its own or navigated to within a Frame.
''' </summary>
Imports Windows.Storage
Imports Windows.Storage.Streams
Imports System.IO.Stream
Public NotInheritable Class MainPage
  Inherits Page
  Public storagefolder As StorageFolder
  Public MyFile As String = "MyFile.txt" ' File Name

Private Sub Button_Click(sender As Object, e As RoutedEventArgs)
    ' Create sample file; replace if exists.
    createfile()
End Sub

Public Async Sub createfile()

'Get the folder pointer we need to use
Dim storageFolder As StorageFolder =
Windows.Storage.ApplicationData.Current.LocalFolder

'File creations
Dim sampleFile As StorageFile = Await storageFolder.CreateFileAsync(MyFile,
CreationCollisionOption.ReplaceExisting)
```

```vbnet
    End Sub

    Private Sub butwritefile_Click(sender As Object, e As RoutedEventArgs)
Handles butwritefile.Click
        writefile()
    End Sub

'subroutine for writing to a file
Public Async Sub writefile()

Dim storageFolder As StorageFolder =
Windows.Storage.ApplicationData.Current.LocalFolder
' Create sample file; replace if exists.

Dim sampleFile As StorageFile = Await storageFolder.GetFileAsync(MyFile)
' Using Buffer to store and do a read before writing this sufficed ' for appending
Dim buffer = Await Windows.Storage.FileIO.ReadBufferAsync(sampleFile)

Dim dataReader As DataReader =
Windows.Storage.Streams.DataReader.FromBuffer(buffer)

Dim text As String = dataReader.ReadString(buffer.Length)

'Prepare to write with string could use a textbox
'Takes Data written/data to write and adds a CR LF
    Await Windows.Storage.FileIO.WriteTextAsync(sampleFile, text & txtdatain.Text
    & vbCrLf)

End Sub

'Button read event
Private Sub butread_Click(sender As Object, e As RoutedEventArgs) Handles
butread.Click

    readfile()

End Sub

'Sub for reading file
Public Async Sub readfile()

    Dim storageFolder As StorageFolder =
Windows.Storage.ApplicationData.Current.LocalFolder
```

```
Dim sampleFile As StorageFile = Await storageFolder.GetFileAsync(MyFile)

Dim buffer = Await Windows.Storage.FileIO.ReadBufferAsync(sampleFile)

'Read whole file
Dim dataReader As DataReader =
Windows.Storage.Streams.DataReader.FromBuffer(buffer)
    Dim text As String = dataReader.ReadString(buffer.Length)
'Write to textbox
txtfile.Text = text
End Sub

End Class
```

Code for the project.

Notice the createfile subroutine requires the Async parameter as do many other routines. Read about Async if you want, I do not plan to go into that concept in this book since it is available in numerous places on the web.

This is a bit different from typical Visual Basic methods for file operations, but it was tested with these parameters and works fine. Also notice, that the libraries are not automatically added. In Visual Basic for Windows when you add a library like Imports System, you get all the objects in the library. Only the specific libraries declared are used.

There is a setup switch in Visual Basic that can add all the libraries after the imports object and make it more like Visual Basic for Windows. It is advised that you keep your code smaller and just use what you need, so you can see why this was done in UWP as a default.

Note: When objects are not recognized, it is apparent you need specific Imports statements or references to declare them.

Note: Alt-Enter when on an error with red lines underneath will show you a lot about what you might need to add or do to get it to work.

Do not forget to add the Imports statements that are required.

GPIOToggle

Program Name:
GPIOToggle

Purpose:
This is an example that will show how to utilize the Raspberry Pi's GPIO electronics.

Tools Needed:
Raspberry Pi 3 B Computer.
You will also need a LED, and 220 Ohm resistor, breadboard, and Jumper wires (solid phone cable will work). A volt-ohm meter can suffice to test where tools are recommended, although having the components is more fun.

Tools Recommended: The Sunfounder kit with Pi Ribbon cable, breadboard, GPI Extension Board, and wire connectors/Jumpers all provided in the package. CanaKit kit in part or whole. CanaKit has a nice case and the things you need, and they also have a component kit and their GPIO extender is more helpful than most. This project uses the Sunfounder Kit since did not have the CanaKit. I will use it no the next one.

Skills Gained:
This will teach the basics of using the GPIO and electronics to turn on a light or LED.

Importance:
The GPIO ports of the Pi are one of the things that are so cool about it!

Description:

We will utilize a button on the screen that can be touched on a touch screen or clicked with a mouse to Toggle a LED.

The main library required besides the UWP-Universal Windows Platform by the Visual Studio 2017 Community is the following:
Imports Windows.Devices.Gpio

The library for GPIO called by the imports statement above should be available in Visual Studio if you selected Universal.

The first thing is to setup your breadboard. This can be more complicated than it should be. There are different names for locations and name of pins, and it's confusing.

Please note the GPIO has a number that is associated with each input and output pin. One example is GPIO Pin 17 which is used to program the 6th pin on the left from the pin connector out. Please review the diagrams that are included.

There are some excellent kits to help save you time as mentioned in the Recommended Tools section. The Sunfounder is the first electronic Raspberry Pi electronics kit I have worked with. The CanaKit offers neat cases and components and is the champion of protecting your Pi.

For Sunfounder, the ribbon cable, and GPIO Extender Board, and breadboard are nice. It is also good to have jumper wires, resistors, switches, motors, and many other sensors to test with.

I have a copy of Sunfounder's illustration of Super Kit V2.0 for Raspberry Pi that came with my kit. It is a helpful manual to get you started and utilizes mostly Raspbian and the libraries. This is a great way to go if you want to experiment with Raspbian, too. The examples from Sunfounder are all in Python, but the kit was excellent for these projects.

I will share the documentation of the board and pictures of the setup using the cable with the projects. Be sure you run the ribbon cable precisely as they have illustrated it. If not, it will not work.

The following diagram shows the ribbon cable and GPI Extension with SunFounder. These kits are not required. It's easier to connect right from the Raspberry Pi's GPIO with the extension to the breadboard and use the jumper wires to resistors, switches, and LEDs. A breadboard extension from the GPIO is beneficial for the electronics projects.

Name	wiringPi Pin	BCM GPIO	GPIO Extention Board		BCM GPIO	wiringPi Pin	Name
3.3V	-	-	3V3	5V0	-	-	5V
SDA	8	R1:0/R2:2	SDA1	5V0	-	-	5V
SCL	9	R1:1/R2:3	SCL1	GND	-	-	0V
GPIO7	7	4	GPIO4	TXD0	14	15	TXD
GND	-	-	GND	RXD0	15	16	RXD
GPIO0	0	17	GPIO17	GPIO18	18	1	GPIO1
GPIO2	2	R1:21/R2:27	GPIO27	GND	-	-	0V
GPIO3	3	22	GPIO22	GPIO23	23	4	GPIO4
3.3v	-	-	3V3	GPIO24	24	5	GPIO5
MOSI	12	10	SPIMOSI	GND	-	-	0V
MISO	13	9	SPIMISO	GPIO25	25	6	GPIO6
SCLK	14	11	SPISCLK	SPICE0	8	10	CE0
0V	-	-	GND	SPICE1	7	11	CE1
ID_SDA	30	0	ID_SD	ID_SC	1	31	ID_SCL
GPIO21	21	5	GPIO5	GND	-	-	0V
GPIO22	22	6	IGPIO6	GPIO12	12	26	GPIO26
GPIO23	23	13	GPIO13	GND	-	-	0V
GPIO24	24	19	GPIO19	GPIO16	16	27	GPIO27
GPIO25	25	26	GPIO26	GPIO20	20	28	GPIO28
GND	-	-	GND	GPIO21	21	29	GPIO29

GPIO Extension Board Pinout graphic by SunFounder

A broad picture of the Sunfounder GPIO Extension Board that attaches to a breadboard. This is convenient and will save you a lot of time testing your applications.

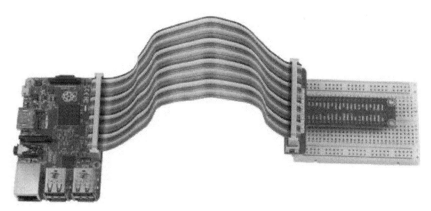

Extension kit from Sunfounder

This is the whole GPI Extension board pictured on the Sunflower site. Notice the cable and how the ribbon cable is configured.

The CanaKit Ultimate pictured next can solve all your problems for this book with one purchase. I like the 3.3V pin that is provided with their T connector, so the power and ground are supplied in the gutters or side column of pins of the board.

CanaKit Ultimate 32 Gig Kit

Be sure you do not bend any of your pins. Be careful inserting and removing the ribbon cable connected to the Raspberry Pi. You should leave this cable in place as much as possible. Once the pins are bent, it will require replacing a pin with a soldering iron or a new Raspberry Pi or kit might have to be purchased.

Also, be particularly careful with the T type connector that goes into the breadboard. For these, examples note Pin 1 on the breadboard lines up with 3v3 on the side when using the Sunfounder. If you have a multimeter or continuity tester, test it.

With the power off, test the pins and be sure they are connected. Just use paperclips with a removed ribbon cable, and verify each GPIO pin from both sides. An audible continuity meter can do this quickly as can a Volt-Ohm meter. If you are not experienced in electronics or with this setup, this is an excellent exercise to help you understand the wiring and pins.

GPOI T-Connector and breadboard

All warnings have been given. Now let's get to it. Power off your Raspberry Pi. Get an LED of any color which is a Light Emitting Diode, preferably one that uses a 220 Ohm resistor. Diodes allow current in one direction, so the orientation of your LED is crucial. Notice one leg is longer than the other to denote the proper application. Each LED has a Cathode and Anode as shown in the representation later in this project.

Anytime you use a Diode or really anything with the Pi; some current limiting device will be needed to keep from burning up the Pi. We will typically use a small resistor. Usually, a 220 Ohm resistor works fine. If the light is bright on the LED, use something with more resistance. Think about a water hose. If you were holding the end of a firehose and turned it on at full blast, it would blow whatever was on the end of it off. Turning the water pressure down, kinking the hose, or some other technique would limit the flow of water.

This is what it would do to the LED. With no resistor, it would run electrons through it so fast it would be very bright and burn out, or the Pi would burn out. Always have the right size resister for an LED and for most components, so you can limit the current. This is like kinking a water hose.

Once you have your Pi and ribbon cable connected, add a resistor and LED as shown.

Note: Your breadboard may be numbered differently.

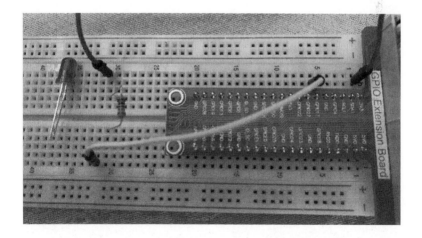

Breadboard with wiring as the project requires

The top wire is going from the breadboard slot 1 and connected on the GPIO connector which is 3.3 volts, to breadboard spot 31 row where a resistor is connected to one of the five connected breadboard spots. The resistors other side or leg goes to the breadboard spot 31 on the other side of the breadboard across the center channel.

Note: The breadboard has a center channel, and no slots are connected between that channel. The five vertical slots are connected. See the diagram of connectivity of a breadboard in the Breadboard Overview section at the back of the book.

The lower or white wire is connected to the Raspberry Pi's pin at GPIO 17. It is at a breadboard spot marked 6 and is connected to breadboard slot #32. This is just to the left of the row hooked into the resistor.

Pin 17 will be the Raspberry Pi's GPIO pin we will utilize in code, and it usually will be high or low at 3.3 volts to 0 volts when it is activated. The next step is to insert the LED. Mine is red, but usually, that does not matter. The LED must work on 3.3 volts and uses a 220-ohm resistor for everything I am describing to work correctly.

LED position and placement

Now insert the LED with the more extended leg toward the GPIO Extender/ribbon cable. One leg will be in line with the resistor on the lower side at breadboard slot #31 and the other at breadboard slot #32 in line with the white jumper cable. Each breadboard may have different numbering.

If you feel you have everything right and the light does not work, power down and flip the LED wires/legs over and retry. The LED has an Anode and Cathode lead that must be connected in the right direction.

Note: Again, the breadboard slot numbers only work if you are using the breadboard and extender as I have it. The resistor and LED are connected in line to the Pi

Notice first the order of the Pins on the Raspberry Pi's GPIO and how Pin 17 is not ordered sequentially as pin 17. These diagrams are imperative for you to get this working right.

I will give you both ways to hook this up on both examples. If you do not have a kit, it will still work fine. You can test it with your volt-ohm meter between GPIO 17 and 3 Volts.

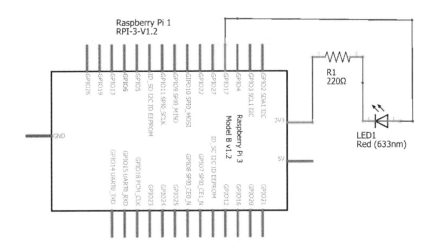

Schematic for lighting it up

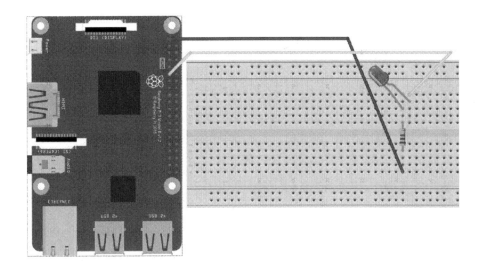

Raspberry Pi Circuit direct to the Pi

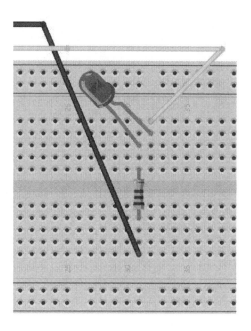

The Breadboard magnified.

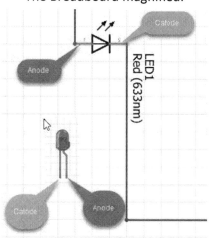

Anode and Cathode of a LED-Light Emitting Diode

Raspberry Pi GPIO Port from the back of the Pi 3 B Touch Screen wired.

This is the GPIO on the Raspberry Pi. This is the same as wiring it through the breadboard. The first pin and the sixth pin are on the component side of the Pi Board.

This will show you the top side of my breadboard using Sunfounders extender kit is the same as wiring to the actual Raspberry Pi GPIO. If you had a volt-ohm tester, you could put it between these pins and read voltage with a button push.

Are you ready to code, this is the easy part?

Open a new Visual Basic Universal project, and setup all the initial settings.

Name this project **GPIOToggle**.

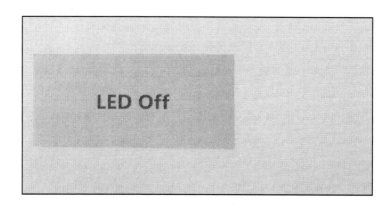

My Pi Touch Screen.

1. Create a button
   a. Content=butNowDoIt
   b. Adjust on screen
2. Grid
   a. Name=MyGrid
   b. Width=(you set it)
   c. Height=(you set it)
   d. Page set same as grid

Add the constants and variables at the top that are used in this class that is below. You must have the Import statement for this to work.

```
Private gpio
Private activepin as GpioPin
Private Const cACTIVE_PIN = 17
```

The constant cACTIVE_PIN is obviously the pin we are planning to toggle. Here is what you should have so far.

```
Imports Windows.Devices.Gpio ' Setup IO and make the library available
Public NotInheritable Class MainPage
  Inherits Page
```

```
Private gpio
Private activepin As GpioPin
Private Const cACTIVE_PIN = 17 ' Active pin that is toggled
```

Now you are ready to design the subroutine that will toggle the LED and change the text on your button. You must check the conditions of the objects and variables to know what the LED status is currently. This will be true for most applications you write.

A check for "nothing" meaning nothing has been setup for the object or the pin in this case. It has not been instantiated, or started and created. Basically, it is empty or null or in a middle state. The pin is initiated in our code. These GPIO pins are not just simple variables, but more complicated objects in the GPIO library with many properties and methods.

Notice the "if...then...else's that check status of the LED. It is checking for an on or off state, and an action is taken. This is really the building block of the Raspberry Pi and Visual Basic code for GPIO and electronics projects.

We can now read a button, input, detect an event, and do another action (redirecting our code flow). In this case, it is a button on the screen. It really does not matter who calls the subroutine, or from where. We just use a subroutine we created to do the activities we want it to accomplish.

```
Private Sub ToggleLED()

    'Check if gpio was already Initiated
    If gpio Is Nothing Then
        gpio = GpioController.GetDefault
    End If

    'Check if LED's pin was already initiated
    If activepin Is Nothing Then
        activepin = gpio.OpenPin(cACTIVE_PIN)
```

```
        activepin.Write(GpioPinValue.Low)
        activepin.SetDriveMode(GpioPinDriveMode.Output)
        butnowdoit.Content = "LED Good"  ' Change button text
    End If

    'Read pin status and invert state
    If activepin.Read = GpioPinValue.High Then
        activepin.Write(GpioPinValue.Low) ' toggle I/O output
        butnowdoit.Content = "LED Off"   ' Toggle button Text
    Else
        activepin.Write(GpioPinValue.High)
        butnowdoit.Content = "LED On"
    End If
End Sub
```

Now all that is left is to add this call to the subroutine in the button click event.

```
Call ToggleLed()
```

This is a subroutine and could be passed with a variable if desired. It also could have been a function that returned a value. In either case, it is a routine that is being used when we call it.

Note: The text wrapping below makes this different than it looks in code. The extra lines will not likely be what you see on your screen. The Private Sub butnowdoit_Click(is on one line in Visual Studio, but not in the real Visual Basic code.

```
Private Sub butnowdoit_Click(sender As Object, e As RoutedEventArgs) Handles butnowdoit.Click
    'Call the Subroutine to toggle the current value of the LED's
    Call ToggleLED()
End Sub
```

Since a lot of new concepts were discussed, I will show as much as is possible. I will include all the code for this project together.

```vbnet
' The Blank Page item template is documented at
https://go.microsoft.com/fwlink/?LinkId=402352&clcid=0x409
''' <summary>
''' An empty page that can be used on its own or navigated to within a Frame.
''' </summary>
Imports Windows.Devices.Gpio
' Setup IO and make the library available
Public NotInheritable Class MainPage
    Inherits Page
    Private gpio     'make it a public object
    Private activepin As GpioPin
    Private Const cACTIVE_PIN = 17  ' Active pin that is toggled


    'Subroutine to toggle LED's or send a pin high or low in
    ' this case Low turns the LED on
    ' Note the LED must be in the right position current will only
    '  flow one way on a diode using DC.
    ' Used the SunFounder kit with breadboard and ribbon
    'cable to make it easier
    Private Sub ToggleLED()

        'Check if gpio was already initialized
        If gpio Is Nothing Then
            gpio = GpioController.GetDefault
        End If

        'Check if LED's pin was already initiated
        If activepin Is Nothing Then
            activepin = gpio.OpenPin(cACTIVE_PIN)
            activepin.Write(GpioPinValue.Low)
            activepin.SetDriveMode(GpioPinDriveMode.Output)
            butnowdoit.Content = "LED Good" ' Change button text
            ' sets the cACTIVE_PIN to LOW really
        End If

        'Read pin status and invert state
        If activepin.Read = GpioPinValue.High Then
            activepin.Write(GpioPinValue.Low) ' toggle I/O output
            butnowdoit.Content = "LED Off"    ' Toggle button Text
        Else
            activepin.Write(GpioPinValue.High)
            butnowdoit.Content = "LED On"
        End If
    End Sub
```

```
Private Sub butnowdoit_Click(sender As Object, e As RoutedEventArgs)
Handles butnowdoit.Click
    'Call the Subroutine to toggle the current value of the LED's
    Call ToggleLED()

    End Sub
End Class
```

This should help to get you on track with these concepts. I also introduced screen changes in the XAML. I will show you the results of the textual XAML file of MainPage.xaml below.

As a last resort, you can change the XAML text; it should be easy to set this up with **Design** mode though. Below is the MainPage.xaml code.

```
<Page
    x:Class="testgpio2.MainPage"
    xmlns="http://schemas.microsoft.com/winfx/2006/xaml/presentation"
    xmlns:x="http://schemas.microsoft.com/winfx/2006/xaml"
    xmlns:local="using:testgpio2"
    xmlns:d="http://schemas.microsoft.com/expression/blend/2008"
    xmlns:mc="http://schemas.openxmlformats.org/markup-compatibility/2006"
    mc:Ignorable="d">

    <Grid x:Name="mygrid" Background="{ThemeResource
ApplicationPageBackgroundThemeBrush}">
        <Button x:Name="butnowdoit" Content="Test LED"
HorizontalAlignment="Left" Margin="30,33,0,0" VerticalAlignment="Top"
Height="172" Width="353" RenderTransformOrigin="0.21,-0.437"
FontWeight="Bold" FontSize="36"/>
    </Grid>
</Page>
```

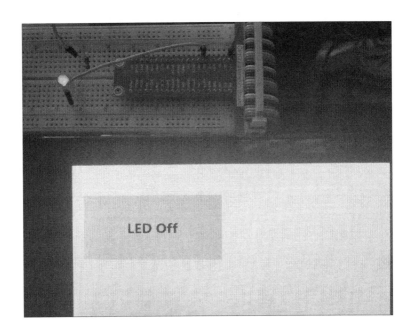

Actual PI Touchscreen and breadboard.

This is what everything should look like if you have the Raspberry Pi 7-inch screen kit and the Sunfounder kit.

GPIOButtonPressed

Program Name:

GPIOButtonPressed

Purpose:

This example demonstrates how you capture an event like an electronic or screen button press input, or a Raspberry Pi GPIO button press. It is then translated it to an output action to turn off and on an LED.

Tools Needed:

Basic Pi Computer.

You will also need a LED, 220 Ohm resistor, breadboard, push button and Jumper wires (solid phone cable will work).

Tools Recommended: CanaKit (CanaKit was used in the example) with a Ribbon cable, breadboard, GPI Extension Board, wire connectors, and electronic components provided.

Skills Gained:

This will teach how to use the GPIO to turn on a light or LED using inputs and outputs.

Importance:

Using the GPIO ports of the Pi are one of the things that are so cool, and this is the primary knowledge you need for most electronic projects. Adding a HAT or board on top can also provide relays that when a pin goes high, can turn on and off high-power items and motors. There MUST be isolation between the Pi and the other devices.

Be careful this kind of activity can fry both you and your Raspberry Pi. This is out of the scope of this book, and you should have engineering or electronics experience before doing anything than what is explained here.

Limitations:

This application is merely toggling the LED with either button push. The electronic button is using the Dispatch timer to check for a switch push. If the button is held down through 2 cycles, it might toggle the LED twice. This is what the Blinky application shown on Python samples does.

You must add a delay counter that provides time for the Electronic button to be pressed and released. After .8 of a second depending on the dispatch timer interval, no new signals to toggle the toggleLed() would be sent. This usually is called bounce. It allows for a delay in electronics between functions. Push buttons require this consideration of bounce be taken. A simple single throw switch will flip on and off. This would make the code easier since it stays in the same position and is not momentary on or off.

Description:

We will utilize a button on the screen that can be touched on a touch screen or clicked with a mouse to Toggle a LED. Additionally, an input pin is scanned from the hardware push button to see if it is pressed. In all cases, it toggles the state of the LED.

There are a few things you will utilize from previous projects. You will use the Dispatch timer to routinely check for a button press causing a state toggle on the GPIO Board. A delay will be added to eliminate bounce.

In this case, we are using the input named GPIO21 on the label, but Pi GPIO pin 5 on the Pi. We are using the same GPIO0, or Pi GPI pin 17 for the output. Either can be an input or output in electronics.

This is a combination of the SimpleTimer sample, and the GPIO LED sample. The toggle routine is identical, and most of the last project is used.

Here is what the finished screen looks like.

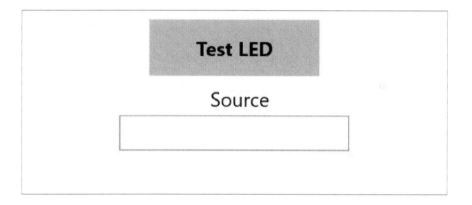

Showing this application while in development.

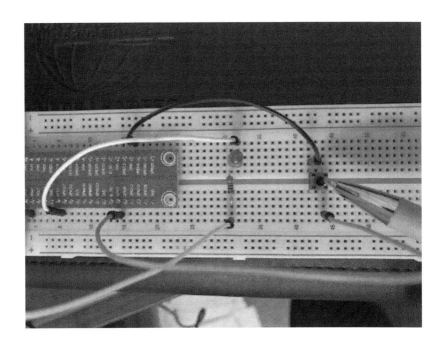

Breadboard wiring red led to pin GPIO21 Pin 5 and Black to Gnd (top Wire)

The miniature push-button is shown at the end of my pin. I have a schematic and breadboard drawing of the circuit at the end of this chapter.

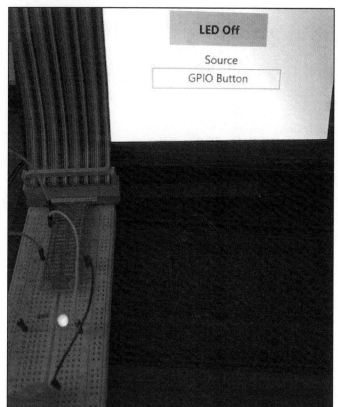

A screen and GPIO Extension after a button push showing the source.

The button has been pushed on the GPIO Board and toggles the LED state.

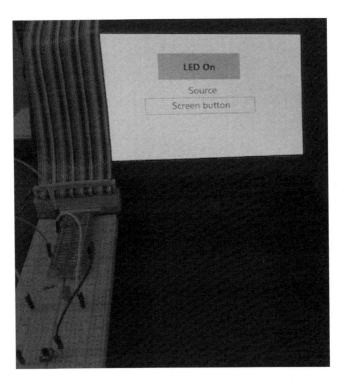

This picture of my Pi this shows button toggle On.

On next push, the light would come on. This program keeps and shows the source of the action that caused the LED toggle. It is easy to see that the program could be used just to turn the LED on or off precisely each time. A standard switch would be On or Off and not momentarily on or off like a push button switch.

Here are the wiring and schematic. At this point

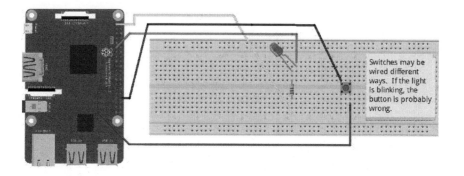

This shows how to wire your Pi.

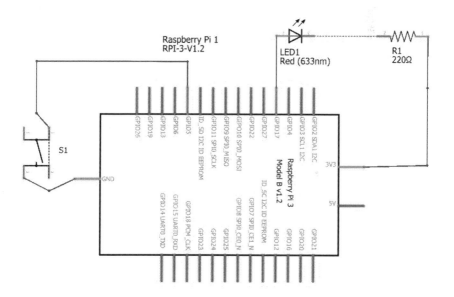

Schematic to the Pi

Ok, let's get started.

Create a new Project and call it **GPIOButtonPress**.

Be sure you use the two import statements, to include the right libraries.

```
Imports Windows.UI

Imports Windows.Devices.Gpio


' The Blank Page item template is documented at
https://go.microsoft.com/fwlink/?LinkId=402352&clcid=0x409
''' <summary>
''' An empty page that can be used on its own or navigated to within a Frame.
''' </summary>
Imports Windows.UI
Imports Windows.Devices.Gpio ' Setup IO and make the library available
Public NotInheritable Class MainPage
Inherits Page
```

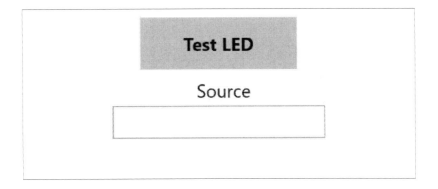

GUI to create is above for this project.

Most of the steps are listed below.

1. Create Button

    a. Name=butnowdoit

    b. Content=**LED Off**

    c. FontSize=36 px

    d. HorizontalAlignment=Center or dual line

    e. Margins=0 0

2. Create Textblock

    a. Name= txtsource

    b. Text=**Source**

    c. Text/Align=Center

        d.   Fontsize=36 px

        e.   Font Alignment=Center

        f.   Margins=0 0

  3.   Create Textbox

        a.   Name=**txtsource**

        b.   Text/Align=Center

        c.   Fontsize=36 px

        d.   HorizontalAlignment=Center or dual line

        e.   Text=

  4.   Grid

        a.   Name=MyGrid

        Note: As it has been for grid and page

The shared variables are below are to be added to the top of the class.

```
Private gpio
Private activepin As GpioPin
Private activepinin As GpioPin    ' Input Pin
Private Const cACTIVE_PIN = 17     ' GPIO 17  Active pin that is toggled
Private Const cACTIVE_PIN_IN = 5 ' Input GPIO 5 Push Button
Dim mytimer As New DispatcherTimer 'Delay Timer
Dim pushbuttondelaytimer As Integer = 0 'Delay counter on push button
Dim GPIOButton As Boolean = False
```

I added the Sub New Routine that is optional, but valuable for starting things up. InitializeComponent() is required as before. This also allows for a place to setup Add Handler and get everything initialized.

```
Public Sub New() '
```

Each action should contain a try...catch error handler, but for our purposes it is okay. Adding the routine for each call will tell which one caused the error so you can correct it and report it.

```
Public Sub New()
```

```
InitializeComponent()
AddHandler mytimer.Tick, AddressOf mytimer_tick
mytimer.Interval = TimeSpan.FromMilliseconds(400) ' adjust to 4/10 of
second
mytimer.Start()
'Prepare GPIO and everything
Try
    'Check if gpio was already initiated
    If gpio Is Nothing Then
        gpio = GpioController.GetDefault
    End If

    ' Get Default working on Input
    If activepinin Is Nothing Then
        activepinin = gpio.openPin(cACTIVE_PIN_IN)
        activepinin.Write(GpioPinValue.Low)
    End If

    'Get default setups in
    If activepin Is Nothing Then
        activepin = gpio.OpenPin(cACTIVE_PIN)
        activepin.Write(GpioPinValue.High)
        activepin.SetDriveMode(GpioPinDriveMode.Output)
        butnowdoit.Content = "LED Off" 'Change button text
    End If
Catch ex As Exception

End Try
End Sub
```

Notice how everything is initialized.

Notice the routine that is a part of the electronic button switch needed a timer. One issue with timers and electronic switches is they can be pushed and released in a momentary switch. Their change of state must happen within the timer event or outside the timing for a new reading of the switch. The button switch push could be missed.

The other issue is that a button could be held down for two cycles of the time event. In this case, I set a 1/10 of a second delay or 100 milliseconds in the timer. It could be lessened to 50, experiment with it once it is working. I also added a .8 second delay (an 8 count at 100 milliseconds) before the electronic switch could be recognized as pushed again.

This delay variable was declared at the top of the class

```
' to use as a second delay counter
Dim pushbuttondelaytimer As Integer = 0
```

I did not want to miss the electronic button switch, so 1 second (1000 milliseconds) was way too long for a delay. If you held the switch button until the light changes, it would work.   I added the routine below to allow it to catch a switch or electronic button push ever 1/10 of a second and delay .8 seconds before allowing another toggleLED() to be called to toggle the LED state. This seems to work fine. You could change the if-then from 8 to 10 or 15 to test this.

Below is the timer event with the delay timer to eliminate double pushes of the electronic button switch.

```
'Timer Event
    Private Sub mytimer_tick(ByVal sender As Object, ByVal e As EventArgs)
        'the if-then below was required to put a delay in the time the
        'electronic button was pushed and released to eliminate double
        'toggles .8 second delay here you can increase
        ' If you hold the button down the LED will blink
        If pushbuttondelaytimer > 8 Then
            pushbuttondelaytimer = 0
        ElseIf pushbuttondelaytimer < 8 And pushbuttondelaytimer > 0 Then
            pushbuttondelaytimer = pushbuttondelaytimer + 1
        Else
            'Input Read on Low it is pushed
            If activepinin.Read = GpioPinValue.Low Then
                ToggleLED("GPIO Button")
                pushbuttondelaytimer = 1
            End If
```

```
        End If
    End Sub
```

There are two other subroutines that do everything. The ToggleLED() and the butnowdoit() event that calls it.

```
Private Sub butnowdoit_Click(sender As Object, e As  RoutedEventArgs) Handles
butnowdoit.Click
        'Call the subroutine to toggle the current value of the LED's
        Call ToggleLED("Screen button")
End Sub
```

The ToggleLED has a parameter (ex: **where As string**) that is passed to allow us to show what event triggered the ToggleLED. This is checking parameters that tell us something about the Raspberry Pi's GPIO input pins, and turn off or on the PI's Output GPIO pins.

```
Simple Toggle of LED
    Private Sub ToggleLED(where As String)
        'Where is used to show source
        txtsource.Text = where  'Show source of LED toggle
        'Check if gpio was already initialized
        If gpio Is Nothing Then
            gpio = GpioController.GetDefault
        End If

        ' Working on it Input
        If activepinin Is Nothing Then
            activepinin = gpio.openPin(cACTIVE_PIN_IN)
            activepinin.Write(GpioPinValue.Low)
        End If

        'Check if LED's pin was already initialized
        If activepin Is Nothing Then
            activepin = gpio.OpenPin(cACTIVE_PIN)
            activepin.Write(GpioPinValue.Low)
            activepin.SetDriveMode(GpioPinDriveMode.Output)
            butnowdoit.Content = "LED Good"  ' Change button text
        End If

        'Read pin status and invert state
        If activepin.Read = GpioPinValue.High Then
```

```
      activepin.Write(GpioPinValue.Low) ' toggle I/O output
      butnowdoit.Content = "LED Off"    ' Toggle button Text
    Else
      activepin.Write(GpioPinValue.High)
      butnowdoit.Content = "LED On"
    End If
  End Sub
```

Just in case here is the MainPage.xaml GUI info below for your review.

```
<Page
  x:Class="GPIOButtonPress.MainPage"
  xmlns="http://schemas.microsoft.com/winfx/2006/xaml/presentation"
  xmlns:x="http://schemas.microsoft.com/winfx/2006/xaml"
  xmlns:local="using:testgpio2"
  xmlns:d="http://schemas.microsoft.com/expression/blend/2008"
  xmlns:mc="http://schemas.openxmlformats.org/markup-compatibility/2006"
  mc:Ignorable="d" Width="800" Height="480" FontFamily="Segoe UI">

  <Grid x:Name="mygrid" Background="{ThemeResource
ApplicationPageBackgroundThemeBrush}">
    <Button x:Name="butnowdoit" Content="Test LED"
HorizontalAlignment="Stretch" Margin="0,21,0,0" VerticalAlignment="Top"
Height="101" Width="313" RenderTransformOrigin="0.21,-0.437"
FontWeight="Bold" FontSize="36"/>
    <TextBox x:Name="txtsource" HorizontalAlignment="Stretch" Height="64"
Margin="0,193,0,0" Text="" VerticalAlignment="Top" Width="424"
FontSize="36" TextAlignment="Center"/>
    <TextBlock x:Name="txtsourcelbl" HorizontalAlignment="Stretch"
Height="46" Margin="0,139,0,0" Text="Source" TextWrapping="Wrap"
VerticalAlignment="Top" Width="128" TextAlignment="Right" FontSize="36"/>
  </Grid>
</Page>
```

Here is all the code together for MainPage.xaml.vb

```
' The Blank Page item template is documented at
https://go.microsoft.com/fwlink/?LinkId=402352&clcid=0x409
''' <summary>
''' An empty page that can be used on its own or navigated to within a Frame.
''' </summary>
Imports Windows.UI
Imports Windows.Devices.Gpio ' Setup IO and make the library available
```

```vb
Public NotInheritable Class MainPage
  Inherits Page
  Private gpio
  Private activepin As GpioPin
  Private activepinin As GpioPin
  Private Const cACTIVE_PIN = 17    ' GPIO ouput pin 17 Active pin that is toggled
  Private Const cACTIVE_PIN_IN = 5  ' Input GPIO 5
  Dim mytimer As New DispatcherTimer
  Dim pushbuttondelaytimer As Integer = 0
  Dim GPIOButton As Boolean = False

  Public Sub New()
    InitializeComponent()
    AddHandler mytimer.Tick, AddressOf mytimer_tick
    'adjusted to 1/10 of a second to be more responsive
    mytimer.Interval = TimeSpan.FromMilliseconds(100) '
    mytimer.Start()
    'Prepare GPIO and everything
    Try
      'Check if gpio was already initialized
      If gpio Is Nothing Then
        gpio = GpioController.GetDefault
      End If

      ' Get Default working on  Input
      If activepinin Is Nothing Then
        activepinin = gpio.openPin(cACTIVE_PIN_IN)
        activepinin.Write(GpioPinValue.Low)
      End If

      'Get default setups in
      If activepin Is Nothing Then
        activepin = gpio.OpenPin(cACTIVE_PIN)
        activepin.Write(GpioPinValue.High)
        activepin.SetDriveMode(GpioPinDriveMode.Output)
        butnowdoit.Content = "LED Off"  ' Change button text
      End If
    Catch ex As Exception

    End Try
  End Sub

  'Timer Event toggled
  Private Sub mytimer_tick(ByVal sender As Object, ByVal e As EventArgs)
    'the if-then below was required to put a delay in the time the
```

```vb
    'electronic button was pushed and released to eliminate double
    'toggles
    ' If you hold the button down the LED will blink
    If pushbuttondelaytimer > 8 Then
        pushbuttondelaytimer = 0
    ElseIf pushbuttondelaytimer < 8 And pushbuttondelaytimer > 0 Then
        pushbuttondelaytimer = pushbuttondelaytimer + 1
    Else
        'Input Read - on Low it is pushed
        If activepinin.Read = GpioPinValue.Low Then
            ToggleLED("GPIO Button")
            pushbuttondelaytimer = 1
        End If
    End If
End Sub

'Simple Toggle of LED
Private Sub ToggleLED(where As String)
    'Where is used to show source
    txtsource.Text = where  'Show source of LED toggle
    'Check if gpio was already initialized
    If gpio Is Nothing Then
        gpio = GpioController.GetDefault
    End If

    ' Working on it Input
    If activepinin Is Nothing Then
        activepinin = gpio.openPin(cACTIVE_PIN_IN)
        activepinin.Write(GpioPinValue.Low)
    End If


    'Check if LED's pin was already initialized
    If activepin Is Nothing Then
        activepin = gpio.OpenPin(cACTIVE_PIN)
        activepin.Write(GpioPinValue.Low)
        activepin.SetDriveMode(GpioPinDriveMode.Output)
        butnowdoit.Content = "LED Good" ' Change button text
    End If

    'Read pin status and invert state
    If activepin.Read = GpioPinValue.High Then
        activepin.Write(GpioPinValue.Low) ' toggle I/O output
        butnowdoit.Content = "LED Off"    ' Toggle button Text
    Else
```

```
        activepin.Write(GpioPinValue.High)
        butnowdoit.Content = "LED On"
    End If
End Sub


Private Sub butnowdoit_Click(sender As Object, e As RoutedEventArgs)
Handles butnowdoit.Click
    'Call the subroutine to toggle the current value of the LED's
    Call ToggleLED("Screen button")
    End Sub

End Class
```

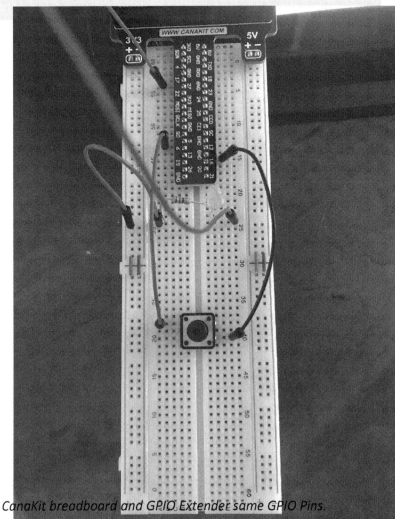

CanaKit breadboard and GPIO Extender same GPIO Pins.

I do like the power and ground provided with this GPIO on the outside. The GPIO extender is an excellent option for these electronic projects. This is a pretty nice.

GPIO Project with LED Turned off by screen button.

GPIO Project turned on and off via GPIO Pin Button.

SQL Server Access and Read

Purpose:

The purpose was to Introduce the way to access and get data from a SQL Server Database.

Tools Needed:

Basic Pi Computer, MS SQL Server and ability to create a table.

Skills Gained:

This shows the basics of getting data from a Microsoft SQL Server database. The select statement is introduced.

Importance:

Obviously, if you want to collect data the microSD chip is not going to hold much due to its size. A Microsoft SQL Server or MySQL database can be maintained and reviewed from anywhere. This remote capability could be helpful in many future applications.

Description:

As a hobby or with data that is not proprietary, this is an excellent way to go. You can even use one of the GoDaddy or WinHost Microsoft SQL Server instances. I am using Winhost to test using my SQL Server Database. Expect a longer response time than when accessing a database that is local, but honestly, it may be unnoticeable. It could be setup locally on your pc.

The preferred way to access a Microsoft QL Server across the internet is not done directly in this manner. It is typically done with SOAP or JSON services in a web service. I wanted to do this with web services. I just did not have a setup that I wanted to support. Webservice is basically an application running on a web server with a more secure connection directly to the database.

This would be acceptable for applications inside the facility or on a secured connection, not on a public network. I will show you the basics of the table used and how a basic query can be done to retrieve the data.

Below is the structure of NameTbl used in this example. It is a fundamental table with no real primary key or indexes. You will have to create this table and have a Microsoft SQL Server database to test this database example.

Column Name	Data Type	Allow Nulls
Fname	varchar(50)	☐
Lname	varchar(50)	☐
Phone	varchar(15)	☑
City	nchar(10)	☑
State	nchar(2)	☑
		☐

NameTbl Table columns from MS SQL Server shown

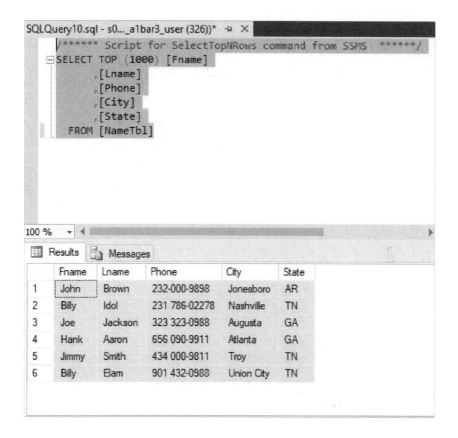

A Microsoft SQL Query and Result of the NameTbl Example

This shows the data that was used for this project and this table NameTbl. The fields are Fname, Lname, Phone, City, and State.

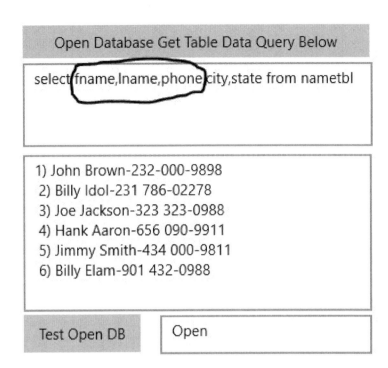

SQL Application Example Utilized in Windows 10 IoT

Notice above that there are 5 fields requested and the fields city and state are not returned. This is intentional; only 6 rows will return and only the first 3 fields. I tried to keep it simple but show the concept. You can change the code and allow more rows to be displayed.

Note: You can consume the data in a GUI control too if you want to take this further.

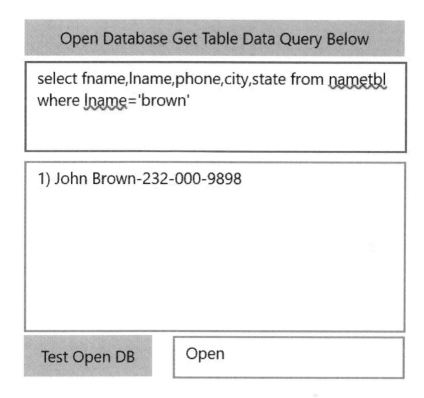

Actual program using where lname='brown'.

This shows a query of just one item using the SQL-statistical query language, where clause and the column lname = 'brown'. It uses a select clause, but it could be an insert or update statement. The lname= statement will return what is true, and you could use a like operator (like '%something').

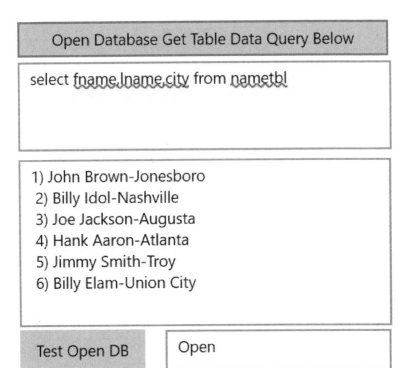

Open Database Get Table Data Query Below

select fname,lname,city from nametbl

1) John Brown-Jonesboro
2) Billy Idol-Nashville
3) Joe Jackson-Augusta
4) Hank Aaron-Atlanta
5) Jimmy Smith-Troy
6) Billy Elam-Union City

Test Open DB	Open

SQL Program using 3 fields and returning all or 6 rows.

The code again is restricting the viewable part to 6 rows and 3 fields. This was done to show the concepts in a textbox.

Before you start coding, you will need to be sure everything is setup right for SQL Server. Without the right Creators version, you may not be able to utilize the Imports statement and libraries.

```
Imports System.Data.SqlClient
```

This statement is critical to getting your application running, and is pictured below.

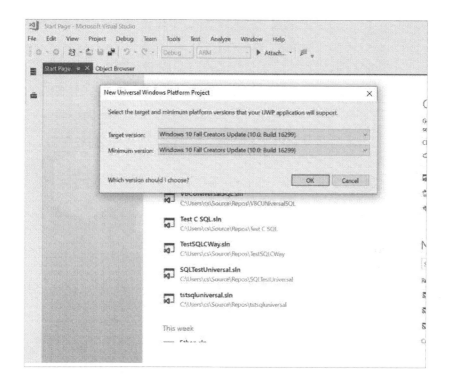

Picking OS System Target Version is required and crucial.

Picking the Versions Target and Minimum is critical for this SQL Server program to work correctly. There may be newer creator editions, but this at a minimum is required to allow for SQL Server to open and to do read/select operations.

The following location was the correct link to update, according to Microsoft. I did not need this.
https://developer.microsoft.com/en-us/windows/downloads/windows-10-sdk.

I wanted to stress the importance of the right version. This version works well, so use it or the newest one. Also, you must create the database table prior to testing this code. Your MS SQL Server must accept a remote login using username and password. MS SQL Server must be setup for this type of access, too.

On to coding, since all of this was done when you created a New Project and named it **SQLUniversalStyle.** Everything else is to be setup as usual, and the grid and page settings are up to you.

Note: This example works equally well in ARM or x64 on an emulator screen.

Let's get started with the screen GUI.

Create each on a new line
1. Create a Button
    a. Name= butGetData
    b. Content=**Open Database Get Table Data Query Below**
2. Create a TextBox
    a. Name=txtquery
    b. Text=
    c. Textwrapping=Wrap
3. Create a Textbox
    a. Name=txtresults
    b. TextWrapping=Wrap
    c. Text=
4. Create a Button
    a. Name=ButOpen
    b. Content=**Test Open Db**
5. Create a TextBox
    a. Name=txtOpen
    b. Text=**Closed**

Ok adding code again you must have only one Import.

```
SQLUniersalStyle                                    ▾  MainPage
1        ' The Blank Page item template is documented at https:/
2        ''' <summary>
3        ''' An empty page that can be used on its own or naviga
4        ''' </summary>
5        Imports System.Data.SqlClient
6        Public NotInheritable Class MainPage
7            Inherits Page
8            Dim CString As String - "SERVER-c99 winhost com:DAT
```

Code window for Imports.

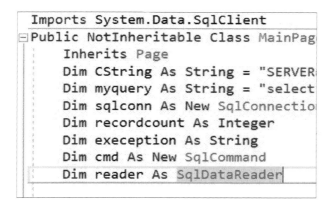

```
Imports System.Data.SqlClient
Public NotInheritable Class MainPag
    Inherits Page
    Dim CString As String = "SERVER
    Dim myquery As String = "select
    Dim sqlconn As New SqlConnectio
    Dim recordcount As Integer
    Dim exeception As String
    Dim cmd As New SqlCommand
    Dim reader As SqlDataReader
```

More startup code to be used in your class.

CString is the hardest thing to get right to set all the parameters right.

Note: I removed the parameters and settings for my database. You will need to add your parameters. Do not forget to remove the < and >.

```
Dim CString As String = "SERVER=<Server
Address>;DATABASE=<Databasename>;USER ID = <DB
USERNAME>;PASSWORD=<PASSWORD>
```

At this point, I am sure you might want to use variables for these to make it easier to read. I tried to lay it out so you could see the whole string. This might be how CString would be if

SERVER= www.sd1.com

DATABASE=myDB

USER ID=JohnBoy

PASSWORD=password1

```
Dim Cstring as String="SERVER=www.sd1.com;DATABASE=myDB;USER
ID=JohnBoy;PASSWORD=password1"
```

Nothing works if the server string in Cstring is incorrect. Test everything with the open command first to see if your strings are correct.

Note: Once this is working try to create a variable and create your CString.

The second statement is the SQL Query itself. This is a Select statement doing read-only. Others should work fine to insert and update if you have the right privileges. The SQL Select Query is in the variable myQuery.

Cstring = "Server=" & server & ";Database=" & ..... and so on

Below is a query that is replaced with the contents of txtquery.text.

```
Dim myquery As String = "select firstname, lastname, workphone from contacts"
```

Typing into the txtquery box and pushing the button control at the top will change the results of your SQL. There is a "try..catch" statement to catch most errors, so you will not cause your computer to shut down.

The database subroutine shows the basics of opening a database.

```
Public Sub opendb(mycon As String)
    'sqlconn As New SqlConnection(CString)
```

```
  Try
      sqlconn.Open()
  Catch ex As Exception
      txtopen.Text = "Failed to Open Database"
  Finally
      txtopen.Text = sqlconn.State.ToString()
  End Try
End Sub
```

This is the heart of the code where it opens and retrieves the select statement. If the database is open, it does not reopen. Opening and closing the database every time can be slow and sometimes unnecessary.

```
Public Sub ExecQuery(Query As String)
    'reset query stats
    recordcount = 0
    exeception = ""
    Dim j As String = ""
    Dim a As String = ""
    Dim i As Integer = 1
    Try
      'Open the Database
      If sqlconn.State.ToString() <> "Open" Then
          opendb("Reserved this for use later-Global now")
      End If

      'Query the Table using variable Query
      cmd = New SqlCommand(Query, sqlconn)
      reader = cmd.ExecuteReader()

      'Was anything retrieved
      If (reader.HasRows) Then

        'Do While Loop Read Until end of Records
        Do While (reader.Read())
          'Column numbers starts at 0
                      j = reader.GetString(0).ToString & " " &
reader.GetString(1).ToString & "-" & reader.GetString(2).ToString

            'String formatting
                a = a & String.Format("{0}) {1} {2} ", i.ToString, j, vbCrLf)
            'Counter for Records
            i = i + 1
```

179

```
                'Limit return of records testing
            If i > 6 Then Exit Do
        Loop
        txtresults.Text = a

    End If
Catch ex As Exception
    'Capture bad here
    exeception = "Exec Query Error" & vbCrLf & ex.Message.ToString
    txtresults.Text = exeception
Finally
    'Close Connection
    If sqlconn.State = System.Data.ConnectionState.Open Then
sqlconn.Close()
    End Try
End Sub
```

Many new concepts have been introduced you may not be familiar with.
A new conditional Do...While...Loop is presented in this project. You can
Exit do, or meet the conditions of the loop to exit the loop. Be careful not
to put yourself in an endless loop in your code.

The I>6 limits the records returned. There are MS SQL Commands that
can also do this limiting which is a better solution. The three fields
returned are shown in this code snippet. You could add one field by
simply adding the following: & "-" & reader.GetString(3).ToString to get
a 4th column or field.

```
'Column numbers start at 0
j = reader.GetString(0).ToString & " " & reader.GetString(1).ToString & "-" &
reader.GetString(2).ToString
```

Notice 0,1,2 with reader.GetString(#), which are the first 3 fields in the
select statement that are returned. They are concatenated by using &
and formatting is being added. Yes, we could use the other formatting
available for a string.

There are screen controls you can populate instead of handling all of this yourself, but you will need more practice and instruction than this example is intended to give.

By watching **sqlconn. state** status you can see if the database is open, and then it can be closed or ignored. Closing the database or any object or variable is standard procedure when you are done, but there are times you may want to keep the database connection open. It depends on your application, and you can do multiple actions prior to closing.

Although I have not opened a MySQL database or another type database with UWP, I would bet it is very similar. I could not find a Visual Basic Example anywhere for UWP and SQL Server, so I wanted to provide one. This code is like normal VB.NET though, so you can use a plethora of examples available online.

There are several ways to work with a Microsoft SQL Server database remotely. This method may be excellent if you can keep it off the public internet. On the open web, your text to connect string is exposed. For logging things like weather or your own personal projects without secure data, it is excellent.

As mentioned, I planned to do a JSON or SOAP example using web services, but I have run out of time and did not have one that I could leave setup. This will be in the next book, I assure you.

Note: Use the butOpen to test your database parameters in this application.

Here is all the code in one place

' The Blank Page item template is documented at
https://go.microsoft.com/fwlink/?LinkId=402352&clcid=0x409

```vb
''' <summary>
''' An empty page that can be used on its own or navigated to within a Frame.
''' </summary>
Imports System.Data.SqlClient
Public NotInheritable Class MainPage
    Inherits Page

    'Removed all parameters here you will need to add  yours
    Dim CString As String = "SERVER=????;DATABASE=????;USER ID =
    ?????;PASSWORD=????"
    'These were my table parameters you will need to add yours
        Dim myquery As String = "select firstname, lastname, workphone from
    contacts"
        Dim sqlconn As New SqlConnection(CString)
        Dim recordcount As Integer
        Dim exception As String
        Dim cmd As New SqlCommand
        Dim reader As SqlDataReader


        Private Sub butgetdata_Click(sender As Object, e As RoutedEventArgs) Handles
    butgetdata.Click
            ExecQuery(txtquery.Text)
        End Sub

        Public Sub ExecQuery(Query As String)
            'reset query stats
            recordcount = 0
            exeception = ""
            Dim j As String = ""
            Dim a As String = ""
            Dim i As Integer = 1
            Try
                'Open the Database
                If sqlconn.State.ToString() <> "Open" Then
                    opendb("Reserved this for use later-Global now")
                End If

                'Query the Table
                cmd = New SqlCommand(Query, sqlconn)
                reader = cmd.ExecuteReader()
                If (reader.HasRows) Then
                    'Read Until end of Records
                    Do While (reader.Read())
                        'Column numbers starts at 0
```

```vbnet
            j = reader.GetString(0).ToString & " " & reader.GetString(1).ToString &
"-" & reader.GetString(2).ToString

                'String formatting
                a = a & String.Format("{0}) {1} {2} ", i.ToString, j, vbCrLf)
                'Counter for Records
                i = i + 1
                'Limit return of records testing
                If i > 6 Then Exit Do
            Loop
            txtresults.Text = a

        End If
    Catch ex As Exception
        'Capture bad here
        exeception = "Exec Query Error" & vbCrLf & ex.Message.ToString
        txtresults.Text = exeception
    Finally
        'Close Connection
        If sqlconn.State = System.Data.ConnectionState.Open Then
sqlconn.Close()
    End Try
End Sub


Private Sub ButOpen_Click(sender As Object, e As RoutedEventArgs) Handles
ButOpen.Click
    Dim sqlconn1 As New SqlConnection(CString1)
    'Testing a connection similar to the open you plan to use
    Try
        sqlconn1.Open()
    Catch ex As Exception
        txtopen.Text = "Failed to Open Database-Modules parameters wrong
these are not the main ones CSTRING1 above"
    Finally
        txtopen.Text = sqlconn1.State.ToString()
        If txtopen.Text = "Open" Then sqlconn1.Close()
    End Try
End Sub


Public Sub opendb(mycon As String)
    Try
        sqlconn.Open()
    Catch ex As Exception
        txtopen.Text = "Failed to Open Database"
    Finally
```

```
        txtopen.Text = sqlconn.State.ToString()
    End Try
  End Sub

End Class
```

There is a lot here to learn and digest here, but it is cool stuff I assure you. This is something even a seasoned programmer might utilize to get them kickstarted. I have used similar code on the Pi using Raspbian and Python.

One new concept is "string.format()". This allows you to setup a format and then you can just place your variables that are to be inserted into the string. "vbCrLf" is Carriage Return Linefeed, "vbCr" is Carriage Return, "vbLf" is line feed, and there are numerous constants already defined in Visual Basic you can use.

```
'String formatting
a = a & String.Format("{0}) {1} {2} ", i.ToString, j, vbCrLf)
```

Glossary

Visual Basic The language this book was created to use. It is one of the Microsoft languages provided in Visual Studio Community.

VB Visual Basic

IoT Internet of things

OS Operating System

UWP Universal Windows Programming – used to program Pi and many other areas like Xamarin that is used on IOS and Android

Universal A programming name for a selected group of XAML type of applications with a reduced subset of objects and references.

PI This merely an abbreviation for the Raspberry Pi.

Raspberry Pi A foundation that provides computer boards for learning and robotics

IDE Integrated Development Environment

Visual Studio An IDE created by Microsoft around 2005 that provides numerous languages. It's debugging, and editing capabilities are outstanding for one.

Community Visual Studio Community is a free version of Visual

Studio. As of this writing, 2017 is the latest version.

GPIO — General Purpose Input Output. This is the reference to the electronic output/input of the Raspberry Pi.

PC — Personal Computer or Computer

Debug Mode — Debug is a way of programming so you can test variables and parameters prior to releasing a program to be sold or used.

Python — A programming language used mostly with Linux, but now used also in many other areas. It is an interpretive programming language.

Raspbian — Default operating system used on the Raspberry Pi. It comes with Libre Office and many programming languages.

SQL — Statistical Query Languages-Database language for selecting, inserting and updating a database and much more.

Breadboard — A breadboard is often used by electronic hobbyist and designers to test their projects.

MS SQL Server — Microsoft main offering for enterprise database solutions.

Resistor — Electronic components that are used to limit current going to other parts. The color code determines how much is restricted.

LED   The light emitting diode is a tiny device that
                       eliminates and has an anode and a cathode.

Windows 10 IoT   A Microsoft operating system mainly used with a
Core   limited subset of windows libraries restricted for
                       use with a few devices and their device libraries.

NOOBS   The startup program that is best to use on microSD.

Handles   Graphics windows or popups have a place where
                       you can move them and make them smaller or
                       bigger. These are called handles.

Bounce   Electronic bounce is a factor added to eliminate
                       switches going through 2 cycles allowing it to
                       consider delays between off and on.

Diagrams

Most of these diagrams have been shown earlier in the book. I wanted to put the primary references here at the end as well, so they would be easy to find.

CanaKit and Sunfounder make some nice kits for the Raspberry Pi. If you order you Pi 3 B or Pi Zero without a kit, you will need to provide several parts that are hard to find for most of us. Heat Syncs, Power Supplies, Cases, MicroSD chips, HDMI Cables, Jumper wires, breadboards, and adapters are not always at my disposal either.

I have mentioned it throughout the text. I use CanaKit kits exclusively for all my projects for cases. All the necessary components are there to protect your Pi. For electronics components and kits, the Canakit offers everything you need in one kit.

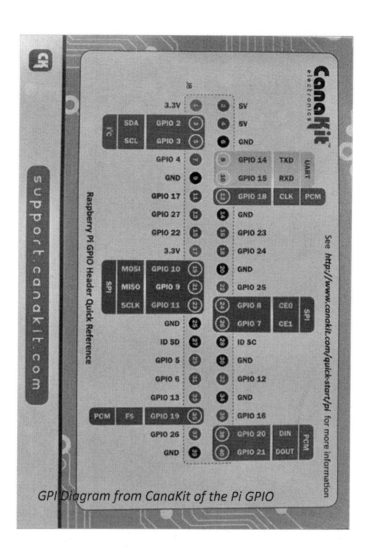

GPI Diagram from CanaKit of the Pi GPIO

Raspberry Pi Board Top

This is the front of my Raspberry Pi Board showing several components.

There are two heat sinks which were added that come in a CanaKit. The 4 USB ports, full HDMI port, Power Port, Ethernet port, speaker port, stereo out, Camera & Monitor ribbon cable interface, and GPIO Pins.

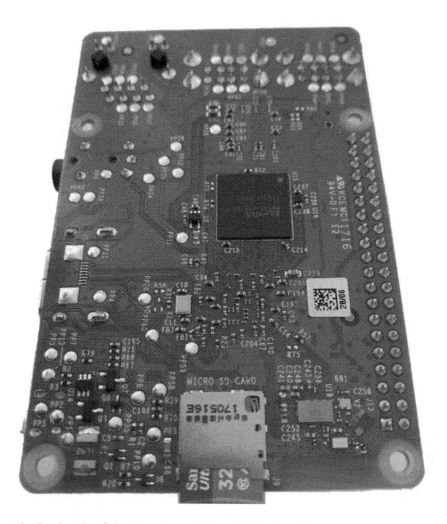

The back side of the Raspberry Pi board showing the MicroSD chip.

Name	wiringPi Pin	BCM GPIO			BCM GPIO	wiringPi Pin	Name
			GPIO Extention Board				
3.3V	-	-	3V3	5V0	-	-	5V
SDA	8	R1:0/R2:2	SDA1	5V0	-	-	5V
SCL	9	R1:1/R2:3	SCL1	GND	-	-	0V
GPIO7	7	4	GPIO4	TXD0	14	15	TXD
GND	-	-	GND	RXD0	15	16	RXD
GPIO0	0	17	GPIO17	GPIO18	18	1	GPIO1
GPIO2	2	R1:21/R2:27	GPIO27	GND	-	-	0V
GPIO3	3	22	GPIO22	GPIO23	23	4	GPIO4
3.3v	-	-	3V3	GPIO24	24	5	GPIO5
MOSI	12	10	SPIMOSI	GND	-	-	0V
MISO	13	9	SPIMISO	GPIO25	25	6	GPIO6
SCLK	14	11	SPISCLK	SPICE0	8	10	CE0
0V	-	-	GND	SPICE1	7	11	CE1
ID_SDA	30	0	ID_SD	ID_SC	1	31	ID_SCL
GPIO21	21	5	GPIO5	GND	-	-	0V
GPIO22	22	6	IGPIO6	GPIO12	12	26	GPIO26
GPIO23	23	13	GPIO13	GND	-	-	0V
GPIO24	24	19	GPIO19	GPIO16	16	27	GPIO27
GPIO25	25	26	GPIO26	GPIO20	20	28	GPIO28
GND	-	-	GND	GPIO21	21	29	GPIO29

This is a copy of the Sunfounder book diagram for pinouts called raspberry Pi Pin Number introduction.

NOTE: This is the GPIO Extender NOT the Pi itself.

GPIO Extension T Board

T part of GPIO Extension board from Sunfounder

Attaches to a Ribbon cable from the Raspberry Pi to create a way to breadboard easily. This has pins on the bottom side that insert into the breadboard.

Please refer to the GPIO Extension Board pinouts and descriptions.

Sunfounder GPIO Extension Kit

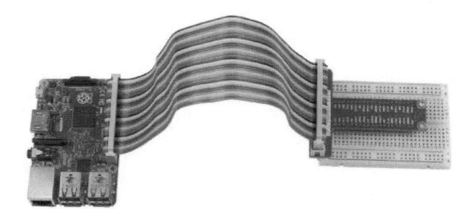

Sunfounder GPIO extender and Breadboard

This is the Sunfounder kit that is around $10 on SunFounder's site. This includes the ribbon cable, connectors, and the T-extender on the breadboard. Some packages include the breadboard, but my cases are usually from CanaKit.

Breadboard & T Extender Diagram

Above are the graphics showing the Raspberry Pi and Sunfounder
extender the way the ribbon cable orients them if plugged into the board
as the previous diagram shows. The top pins on the PI basically line up
with the top pins of the GPIO Extender.

To get more familiar. While power is off, use a continuity or volt-ohm
meter to check resistance, using a paperclip on the ribbon cable to be

sure you understand the pin out. The top right pin on the Pi should show no resistance to the top right pin on the breadboard related to the extender.

CanaKit Ultimate Kit

CanaKit Pi 3 Ultimate Starter Kit -32 Gig Edition.

The beauty of this kit is that is really has everything needed to do all the projects in the book. Just like the previous example mentioned test the pins to be sure you understand them. Use a continuity meter to be sure. http://www.Canakit.com

CanaKit Pi GPIO Board Bundle

This is another kit if you already have the case and a Pi.

I prefer the more CanaKit Ultimate kit with everything. This is a good kit if you already have a Raspberry Pi and case.

Breadboard Overview

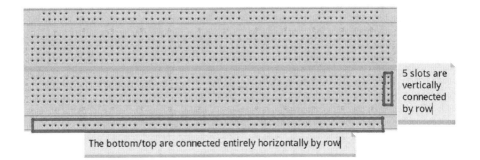

5 slots are vertically connected by row

The bottom/top are connected entirely horizontally by row

A standard breadboard with continuity connections shown.

Web Links

Book Info-http://a1entities.com/2018/02/raspberry-pi-and-visual-basic/

Hello Pi Code-https://github.com/shacksbiz/VB-Universal-Hello-Pi/

Authors Email: cs@a1entities.com

Notes

Printed in Great Britain
by Amazon